Performance Power

Edited by Joss Bennathan

Published by Heinemann Educational Publishers
Halley Court, Jordan Hill, Oxford OX2 8EJ
A division of Reed Educational and Professional Publishing Ltd

OXFORD MELBOURNE AUCKLAND
JOHANNESBURG BLANTYRE GABORONE
IBADAN PORTSMOUTH (NH) USA CHICAGO

05 04 03 02
10 9 8 7 6 5 4 3

ISBN
0 435 23332 7

ACKNOWLEDGEMENTS
The publishers gratefully acknowledge the following for permission to reproduce
copyright material. Every effort has been made to trace copyright holders, but in some
cases has proved impossible. The publishers would be happy to hear from any
copyright holder that has not been acknowledged.

Cover design by Miller Craig and Cocking
Cover photograph by Kelly Mooney/CORBIS
Typeset by Tek-Art
Printed and bound in UK by Clays Ltd, St Ives plc

Tel: 01865 888058 www.heinemann.co.uk

Thanks to:

Paul Moody, Victoria Pembroke and Carole Pluckrose for providing ideas for extracts and activities.

Joan Walker, Elliott Young and Charlie Adams for reading the manuscript and extracts to establish length, and for helping me realise what made sense and what didn't, what was accessible and what wasn't.

Many GCSE Drama students over the years, especially those in Tower Hamlets, Newham, Barking & Dagenham and Redbridge who responded with such enthusiasm and creativity to the extracts featured in this book.

Shirley Wakley and Charlotte Corser at Heinemann for commissioning the collection and all their support since then. Charlotte Barrow for being a very incisive and thorough copy editor.

Most of all, to all the overworked and undervalued Drama teachers who continue to inspire their students with high expectations of what they should be offered and what they can achieve.

TO MY PARENTS

Contents

Section B: Performance

Introduction for GCSE Drama Students

This book will help you to:
- develop and improve your skills as an actor
- create characters different from yourself
- communicate with other actors
- understand how plays are put together and how to create the effects that will move the audience in the way you want them to be moved.

All this is useful if you are improvising and devising your own work, if you are rehearsing and performing existing scripts and if you are writing reviews of plays you have seen.

This book features thirty-two plays. In Section A these are short extracts, with activities to help you develop Drama skills, knowledge and understanding. In Section B there are six short plays (or extracts from and adaptations of longer plays), suitable for performance in small groups. These plays, from different places and times, use various styles and conventions and explore many themes.

Drama is about doing but it is also about reflecting and evaluating. Some of the extracts have been chosen for you to perform. Others have been selected as a stimulus for improvised work. Some will enable you to discuss and analyse different conventions, genres and styles of play, now and in the past.

You can work through the book or dip in and out, using the activities and ideas to apply to other plays that you are studying or to your own improvised work. Whichever way you use this book, you will develop new ways of working, new skills and a greater understanding of how Drama works; all this will help you to improve your own GCSE Drama performance power.

Section A: Elements of Drama

A1: Moving

This chapter shows you how to use your body to communicate. If you have done Drama for any length of time, you'll know that body language is an important way of communicating what a particular character is like. How people move, stand and sit reveals a great deal about their mood and about how the characters feel about themselves and the world they live in.

1 Work in a pair so that you can monitor and advise each other. Take it in turns to:

- move as if it is a freezing cold day
- move as if it is a hot and sweaty day
- move as if you are a very old person
- move as if you are trying to sneak in late at night without being heard or discovered.

Give feedback to your partner by offering three specific points about what has altered; for example, do they walk faster or slower? Is the body tense or relaxed? Do they look straight ahead, from side to side, or down? There is no right or wrong answer. The point is to identify what makes that state, and the movement that results from that state, different from your partner's normal movement.

2 Different people move in different ways and, when walking, 'lead' from different parts of the body. See if you can identify which part of your body you lead from. It may be easier for your partner to observe and tell you. First, walk as normally as possible around the studio. Next, adapt your own movement by imagining that you have a string pulling from your head, then your chest, then your hips, then your knees. Finally, try walking as if your legs are heavy, then as if your feet are light. Discuss what sort of characters and situations each different way of moving suggests.

The process you have begun in the previous two activities is called *physicalisation*. To develop your understanding of this, read the extract from the play *Gum and Goo*.

> *Gum and Goo* was written by Howard Brenton in 1969. The characters
> are all eleven or twelve. The play was written to be performed with no
> set. It requires bold physicalisation as there is nothing but the actors'
> bodies to tell the audience who the characters are.

 ## Gum and Goo

As the audience come in, G, P and M are playing touch-he, in a circle.
The game goes on for a while.
A plastic football's thrown into the circle.
They pick it up, throw and bounce it about, off the walls, on the ceiling,
*   it's fun.*
It stops being fun. G and P begin to hog the ball.
Piggy in the middle starts. It's fair at first.
But M gets stuck in the middle.
G and P torment M, hide the ball behind their backs, hold it above M's
*   head. M goes on tiptoe to try and get it.*
Suddenly, G throws the ball to M.
Delighted, M throws the ball to P, to start the piggy game again.
But G and P play dead, let the ball roll away.
M tries again to get them to play, but they just stand still.
M gives up, sad. Sits down, lets the ball roll away.
Stands up, turns away, sucks thumb.

---

3 In a group of three, stage this scene in the following ways:

- Experiment with how you use space. If G and P are close to M, is
  that more threatening or less so?
- Try playing different parts. Does the scene work best if M is the
  smallest of the three performers, or the tallest, or doesn't it
  make any difference?
- Make a note of how you (or one of the other performers) alter
  your own way of moving to create a convincing, if cartoon-like,
  eleven or twelve year old.

- Try playing the scene as six year olds instead of eleven year olds. What difference – if any – does that make to how you move?
- Use the movement as the beginning of a scene, adding words so that you develop the story.

In *Gum and Goo*, the actors play the same character throughout the play. In some plays, the actors must be able to physicalise all sorts of different characters in order that they can transform from one character to another (and often back again), without changing costume and without leaving the stage.

The second extract, from *Bouncers* (written in 1983 by John Godber) uses **transformation**. It shows how, without props, costumes or scenery, a small group of actors can represent various different people in different locations. Although the play was written for four male actors, the scene creates exaggerated stereotypes of both genders, so there is no reason why four girls, or a mixed group, shouldn't enact it. Prepare for reading and staging the scene with the following activities:

4   In a group of four, make a list of different stereotypes. Then choose four from the list and create a series of solo frozen pictures showing each stereotype. Help each other to make the physicalisation as bold and exaggerated as possible.

Number each image from one to four. Develop your physical control by transforming first to a count of ten, then to a count of five, then from one to the other on the snap of the fingers or the clap of a hand. (You should take as long as the count or clap to complete the transformation, so that it moves slowly, at a medium pace or instantly.) To begin with, go through the images in numerical order. Then assign one of the group to shout out numbers at random, so that you transform back and forward.

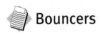 **Bouncers**

The actors become the lads getting ready for the big night out. They all stand in a row and check the various parts of their bodies.

ERIC   Hair?

LES   Check.

JUDD   Tie?

LES   Check.

ERIC   Aftershave? Cliff Richard uses this.   5

ALL   *(sing) Got myself a sleeping walking . . .*

RALPH   Check.

ERIC   Talc on genitals?

LES   Check.

ERIC   Clean underpants?   10

RALPH   Well . . .

LES   They'll do.

ERIC   Money?

JUDD   Double check.

LES   Condoms?   15

ERIC   Checkaroonie.

JUDD   Breath?

They all breathe out and try and smell their own breath.

ALL   Ugh! Beer should drown that.

JUDD   Right. That's it then. We're ready. Catch the bus at the end of our street.   20

RALPH   Ding ding.

LES   Fares please.

ERIC   Bollocks.

JUDD	Get down town to start the pub crawl. When we get there it's packed already. I see me mates. Baz, Jerry an' Kev an' me into the Taverners.

25

During the following sequence the lads attempt to get served. Their actions should convey the bustling, pushy atmosphere of a pub.

JUDD	Four pints, please!
ALL	*(as they down the first pint of the evening)* ONE!!
LES	Course I'm eighteen.
ERIC	Get some crisps.
JUDD	Four bags of beef.
RALPH	Look at tits on that.
ALL	*(to audience)* Social comment.
JUDD	Four pints, pal.
ALL	TWO!!
RALPH	Hey, who's pushing?
ERIC	Are you being served?
LES	Hey up, bastard.
RALPH	Four more pints, pal.
ALL	THREE!!
JUDD	Got any pork scratchings?
ERIC	Hey, watch me shirt.
RALPH	Look who's pushing?
LES	Packed in't it?
JUDD	Let me get to them bogs.
ERIC	Excuse me.
RALPH	Four pints.
ALL	FOUR!!

30

35

40

45

JUDD	And a whisky, love, please.	50
ALL	FIVE!!	
RALPH	Are we off?	
ERIC	D'you think we'll get in?	
JUDD	Should do.	
LES	Hope there's no trouble.	55
ERIC	There's four of us.	
ALL	Yeah.	
RALPH	Come on. Let's get down there, pick something up. Right.	
ALL	Right.	60
ERIC	Hang on.	
LES	What?	
ERIC	Piss call.	
ALL	Oh yeah.	

They all turn their backs as if peeing and then turn back to face the audience.

JUDD	We'd better split up.	65
LES	Why?	
JUDD	The Bouncers.	
ERIC	Don't let you in. In groups.	
RALPH	OK. Me and Kev. Right.	
JUDD	Yeah. And me and . . . *(realising who he's paired off with)* Oh shit!	70

Just as they are about to move away they all freeze. Pause. They become the girls. Eric (Maureen), Les (Rosie), Judd (Elaine), and Ralph (Suzy) all stand together in a circle having a laugh and a drink in a pub. They are all dressed up in their brand new clothes ready for the night out. This should be

communicated to the audience through their
actions. They introduce themselves one by one.

ERIC Maureen. Massive but nice. Fat but cuddly. Not a bag, but likes a drink and a laugh. A bit busty.

LES Rosie. Birthday today. Tall and slim, hair all 75 permed. I had it done at Barbara's.

ERIC It's nice. It really suits you.

LES Thank you.

ERIC Cow.

LES I've had a drink. I feel a bit tiddly. Hey, it 80 will end in tears. Hello luv.

ERIC Hello.

LES Have you lost a bit of weight?

JUDD Plain Elaine.

ERIC AND LES It's a shame. 85

JUDD Left school at sixteen with one **CSE** in metalwork. I'm on the dole.

ERIC AND LES It's such a shame.

JUDD Enjoys a good night out but doesn't expect to get picked up though. Handy in 90 a fight . . . come here ya bastard.

RALPH Rosie, Maureen, Elaine . . .

ALL Suzy . . .

RALPH . . . sexy . . . I've got stockings on under my dress. Do you wanna look? You cheeky 95 getts! Go on then. Anybody's for half a lager. Goes under the sunbed . . . brown

---

CSE Certificate of Secondary Education (together with O levels, which were a higher academic qualification, replaced by GCSE).

all over. I bet you would fancy it, big boy. Ooh, he's nice that one.

LES	I'll say he is. Yeah. Right. Who wants what? 100
JUDD	I'll have a pint of Guinness . . . no, only a joke. I'll have a brandy and lime.
ERIC	Well. I'll have a lager and black because if I have any more I'll be on my back.
LES	As usual. 105
ERIC	You cheeky sod.
LES	Sorry.
RALPH	I'll have a *Pina Colada*.
ERIC	Christ. Listen to her.
RALPH	Well I'm eighteen. 110
LES	She doesn't bloody care. I feel a bit sick.
ERIC	You'll be alright when we get down there.
LES	Are we getting the bus?
RALPH	Well, I'm not walking it in these shoes.
ALL	They're lovely. 115
RALPH	I know.
JUDD	I'm gonna put a record on.
ALL	Ya da da da da da da ya da da da da.

Judd walks up to an imaginary jukebox, represented by Eric. Les and Ralph join Judd around the jukebox.

RALPH	Put that on 3A. I like that.
JUDD	No. It's crap. 120
LES	I think you should put Wham on.
JUDD	I'm putting on a funky disco record.
RALPH	I'm afraid you are not, because I like this one here by Sister Sledge. *(singing, as if the*

record) I was walking down the street one day, I heard a voice, I heard a voice . . .
(repeats as if the record is sticking)

Sudden blackout and freeze. The actors walk to the side of the stage. A dark and foreboding sound filters out from the speakers. The pace has been fast and hectic up until this point, but now the stage is quite still. We are outside the club. Eerie, disturbing music plays as we move into a mime sequence during which the bouncers come to life. During this sequence each actor should create and display a kind of larger-than-life character for each bouncer. It is at this point that the individual characteristics of each bouncer are established. Ordinary mannerisms and gestures are grotesquely exaggerated as one by one, the bouncers step forward to introduce themselves.

In the same group of four:

5   List the different characters that appear. Choose an appropriate action or gesture for each character.

6   Note when the characters talk directly to the audience. Note when they respond to invisible characters and who those characters are. List the different events that are communicated using mime.

7   Stage the scene, using the bold physicalisation from Activity 4 and the actions and gestures from Activity 5 to help create larger-than-life characters.

8   Use the transformation principle to create a scene of your own. Show the scene.

Finally, working on your own:

9   Make notes on what you have discovered about physicalisation and transformation, based on your own practical work and your observations of other groups' work.

Keep these notes to use as a resource whenever you begin creating a new character, either in your improvised work or when working on a script.

A2: Breathing

Breathing is automatic. You don't have to think about the action. But – and you'll know this if you've done any singing – you need to breathe differently if you want to be heard and understood on stage. This chapter shows you how to do this.

The most important muscle for an actor is the diaphragm, between the chest and the abdomen. The following activities help to exercise the muscles that support your voice and breathing so that you can control your voice and make it do what you want on stage.

1 Stand with your feet as wide apart as your hips and with your knees unlocked. (This stops you from tensing up and, incidentally, is a good thing to do just before you go on stage if you are feeling nervous.) Close your eyes to help your concentration. Place your hands on your lower belly. Breathe in slowly on a count of five. Feel your chest cavity expand as the air fills it. Hold for a count of five. Now breathe out on the same count. Repeat this several times until you establish a rhythm. Do the same for a count of ten. Next – if you can – for a count of fifteen.

2 Breathe in. Hum as you breathe out, then open your mouth. The sound will become an 'aaaah'. Repeat a few times, varying the pitch each time.

The following extract is a speech from *Richard II*, which William Shakespeare wrote in the 1590s. The title character is being forced to abdicate and hand over his crown to the man who has defeated him in battle. The language is complex but do not worry if there are words that you do not understand. Use it simply as an exercise in breathing.

 ## Richard II

RICHARD   **Alack**, why am I sent for to a king /
Before I have shook off the regal thoughts
Wherewith I reigned? // I hardly yet have learned
To **insinuate**, flatter, bow, and bend my knee. //
Give sorrow leave a while to tutor me   5
To this **submission**. // Yet I well remember
The favours of these men: / were they not mine? //
Did they not **sometime** cry 'All hail!' to me? //
So **Judas** did to Christ: / but he in **twelve**
Found truth in all but one; / I, in twelve thousand,   10
none. //
God save the King! // Will no man say amen? //
Am I both priest and **clerk**? // Well, then, amen. //
God save the King, although I be not he; /
And yet amen, if Heaven do think him me. //
To do what service am I sent for hither? //   15

Alack like 'Alas', an expression of sadness; **insinuate** to creep;
Give sorrow leave a while allow Sorrow some time; **submission** surrender;
sometime once; **Judas** Judas Iscariot, who betrayed Jesus;
twelve i.e. the twelve disciples;
clerk employed to speak the responses to the priest's prayer.

---

3   The speech is marked at the end of each sentence (//). Breathe in.
Now use the breath (all of it) to chant the sentence, all on one
note. Breathe in again. Now chant the next sentence. And so on.
Don't worry for now about having to pause at the end of each
sentence while you breathe in.

Now do the same thing again, but this time don't chant the
speech: instead, speak it. Next, take a 'catch breath' so that you
pause as briefly as possible before beginning the next sentence.
You will notice that if you breathe correctly – that is, at the end of

each sentence (//) or long phrase(/) – it not only helps you speak but also helps make sense of the speech because you are using your breath to support the punctuation of the speech. It also means that the breathing is corresponding to the thought patterns of the character.

4 Choose another speech from this book (or elsewhere) and mark it in the same way (using pencil marks unless you are working on a photocopy). It doesn't have to be a speech in verse, but it should have longer sentences than occur in everyday speech, so that you develop better breath control.

A3: Speaking

This chapter will help you develop your voice for use on stage. In real life, most of us do not articulate clearly. This means we swallow some of our words, or don't sound the ends of them properly. If this happens when performing, the audience will find it hard to understand what the character is saying.

Just as breathing requires you to exercise your diaphragm, so you also need to give the muscles that support your voice a workout, in particular the tongue, the cheeks and the lips. The first activity exercises those muscles.

1 Massage your face all over with your hands.

- Screw up your face very small and tight as if you were sucking a lemon. Then make your face as wide as possible. Repeat this five times.
- Pout then blow through your lips – you will find the sound that comes out is something like a donkey or a small motorbike.
- Repeat the following tongue twisters several times, as fast as possible, exaggerating your lip movements and sounding all the ends of words clearly. In the first tongue twister, say the sound rather than the letter ('tuh' not 'tee' etc.).

    T-t-t d-d-d c-c-c g-g-g p-p-p b-b-b

Particularly the tip of the tongue, the lips and the teeth

Betty bought a bit of butter

Red lorry yellow lorry

Unique New York

She sells sea shells on the seashore. The shells she sells are sea shells I'm sure.

- Hum a song of your choice, then sing it, with your tongue on your lips. Then speak the words to it, loud and clear.

The next extract is a speech from *Under Milk Wood*, a play that the poet Dylan Thomas wrote for radio and that was first broadcast in 1954.

Under Milk Wood

FIRST VOICE Lord Cut-Glass, in his kitchen full of time,
squats down alone to a dogdish, marked Fido,
of peppery fish-scraps and listens to the
voices of his sixty-six clocks – (one for each
year of his loony age) – and watches, with   5
love, their black-and-white moony loudlipped
faces tocking the earth away: slow clocks,
quick clocks, pendulumed heart-knocks,
china, alarm, grandfather, cuckoo; clocks
shaped like Noah's whirring Ark, clocks that   10
bicker in marble ships, clocks in the wombs of
glass women, hourglass chimers, tu-wit-tu-
woo clocks, clocks that pluck tunes, Vesuvius
clocks all black bells and lava, Niagara clocks
that **cataract** their ticks, old time-weeping   15

cataract pour down in a rush, like a waterfall.

clocks with ebony beards, clocks with no
hands forever drumming out time without
ever knowing what time it is. His sixty-six
singers are all set at different hours. Lord Cut-
Glass lives in a house and a life at siege. Any   20
minute or dark day now, the unknown enemy
will loot and savage downhill, but they will
not catch him napping. Sixty-six different
times in his fish-slimy kitchen ping, strike,
tick, chime and tock.   25

2   Read the speech aloud, slowly, making sure you exaggerate your
    lip movements and sound the end of each word clearly. Read it
    again, faster, but still making sure you sound the words clearly.
    Don't forget to breathe properly as well!

3   Choose another speech from this book, or from a play you are
    studying or rehearsing, and try Activity 2 on it. Choose a speech
    that the character would speak very fast, because that's when it
    gets hardest to understand what someone is saying.

Working on breathing and speaking often makes people feel self-
conscious at first. However, regular use of the activities in this chapter
and Chapter A2: Breathing will improve your ability to speak with
confidence and clarity, whatever character you are playing.

A4: Connecting

This chapter shows you how you can use your own experience to build
a bridge between you and the character you are portraying. It will
show you how to make an imaginative leap from your own life into
whatever the character is experiencing.

Plays often feature characters in extreme or life-threatening
situations. Two examples follow.

King John

CONSTANCE Grief fills the room up of my absent child,
      Lies in his bed, walks up and down with me,
      Puts on his pretty looks, repeats his words,
      Remembers me of all his **gracious** parts,
      Stuffs out his vacant garments with his form. 5
      Then have I reason to be fond of grief?
      Fare you well. Had you such a loss as I,
      I could give better comfort than you do.

      She unbinds her hair.

      I will not keep this form upon my head
      When there is such disorder in my wit. 10
      O Lord! My boy, my Arthur, my fair son!
      My life, my joy, my food, my all the world!
      My widow-comfort, and my sorrows' cure!
      Exit.

Remembers reminds; **gracious** graceful.

himself) is twenty three. The play takes place when the family is cooped up together on a summer holiday. As the title suggests, the play takes place in the course of twenty four hours. Tyrone, the father, is an elderly and bitter actor who quarrels constantly with Jamie, his elder son. Both are alcoholics. Mary, the mother, is a morphine addict. Edmund, the younger son, has just been diagnosed as suffering from tuberculosis which, in those days, was often fatal. None of the family is willing or able to talk about all their addictions or ailments. After a quarrel with his father, Edmund has gone for a walk late at night. He makes this speech just after he has returned home.

Long Day's Journey Into Night

EDMUND   The fog was where I wanted to be. Halfway down the path you can't see this house. You'd never know it was here. Or any of the other places down the avenue. I couldn't see but a few feet ahead. I didn't meet a soul. Everything looked and   5 sounded unreal. Nothing was what it is. That's what I wanted – to be alone with myself in another world where truth is untrue and life can hide from itself. Out beyond the harbour, where the road runs along the beach, I even lost the   10 feeling of being on land. The fog and the sea seemed part of each other. It was like walking on the bottom of the sea. As if I had drowned long ago. As if I was a ghost belonging to the fog, and the fog was the ghost of the sea. It felt   15 damned peaceful to be nothing more than a ghost within a ghost.

He sees his father looking at him with mingled worry and irritated disapproval. He grins mockingly.

Don't look at me as if I'd gone nutty. I'm talking
sense. Who wants to see life as it is, if they can
help it? It's the **three Gorgons** in one. You look in   20
their faces and turn to stone. Or it's **Pan**. You see
him and you die – that is, inside you – and have to
go on living as a ghost.

---

three Gorgons mythical monsters in Greek legend; one look from them turned a
person to stone;
Pan a Greek god, a man with the horns, ears and hooves of a goat, who played the
pipes and would suddenly appear to travellers, terrifying them.

Read both speeches aloud, then choose one to explore, using the
activities which follow. Pick the speech with which you feel the
strongest personal connection, regardless of whether you are male or
female.

1 Who is the character and what situation are they in? List what
   you know, based on the speech and the situation described
   above. Do not be afraid of stating the obvious, e.g. 'Constance is
   a woman'.

2 What do you imagine it feels like to be in that situation? Write a list
   of feelings or images.

3 What is there in your experience that connects with what this
   character is experiencing? You don't know what it's like to be a
   queen in the twelfth century or a young man in America early in
   the last century, but you do know what it is like to:

   • have lost something or someone very important to you (loss
     does not have to mean death)
   • experience hostility
   • feel no one understands your situation
   • feel frustrated or powerless.

   This is called a ***personal source***.

   Write a paragraph describing a situation you have experienced
   which connects with the character whose speech you have chosen.

Write in the present tense – 'I am sitting in my bedroom' not 'I was sitting in my bedroom'. Concentrate on what you could see, smell, touch, taste and feel in the situation you are describing, rather than on the emotion you were experiencing.

(If you have a particularly painful or personal situation or experience in mind, you should think about whether you want to remember it, or use it in this activity. You should also think about whether you would feel comfortable telling others about it, or allowing them to read it. If the answer is 'No' then don't use that experience, or else negotiate that you do not have to share the experience.)

4 Read your paragraph to yourself, or aloud, before reading your chosen speech aloud. Ask a partner to listen to the speech so that they can tell you what emotion has been communicated.

You can apply these activities to any character in any play. No matter how different a character is from you, there is always something that has happened to you that will enable you to connect with what the character is experiencing. **Empathy** (which means discovering and using what you find you have in common with a character) will improve your performance.

A5: Communicating

Often, an actor will know *how* a character speaks – not the accent or dialect, but the tone of voice, and whether this is sad or angry or deliriously happy. This chapter explores *why* a character speaks, that is, what they want to communicate.

1 Select one of the following lines:
  • You won't believe what I've just seen.
  • Give me the money.

Choose an emotion that you think fits the line. Try saying it as if you are:

- very angry
- very excited
- very miserable
- very nervous.

That's *how* the line might be spoken. Now think of *why* it might be said in this way. To do this, invent a character to say the line and the situation in which they might say it. For instance, the first line might be an office worker who wants *to gossip* because they have just seen the boss at lunch with a junior worker; or it might be spoken by a child who wants *to warn* their family that there are hideous aliens landing their spaceship in the back garden. The second line might be spoken by a beggar who needs *to ask for help* because they have no money for food; alternatively, it might be spoken by someone who is holding up a bank and wants *to threaten* a cashier.

It is up to the actor, as the interpreter of the text – the person who has to make the character come to life – to choose an **intention**, a reason for the character to speak. (Some people refer to *motivation* or an *aim* or an *objective*.) To gossip, to warn, to ask for help, to threaten – the actions suggested in Activity 1 – are examples of intentions; you may have noticed that these are all verbs, because an intention is always expressed as 'to . . .'.

In any speech or scene, there may be several right choices as to an intention and several wrong ones. The next extract explores this.

This speech comes from the only twenty-first-century play in this collection, *Kiss Me Like You Mean It* by Chris Chibnall, written in 2001. Tony is talking to Ruth. They have just met at a party. Their respective girlfriend and boyfriend are both at the same party. Ruth's boyfriend wants to marry her, but she is not sure. Tony would not normally dare to say the sort of thing he says in this speech, but an old man has recently advised him to 'grab life by the collar'.

Kiss Me Like You Mean It

Tony takes a deep breath.

TONY   Listen . . . I need to . . . Um . . . Say . . . I mean . . . I
know we only met earlier . . . And I nearly set you
on fire . . . And we're both going out with people.
Obviously that's quite tricky. But . . . Well . . . You
are the most beautiful woman I have ever laid eyes   5
on in my entire life. I saw you and my heart leapt.
You make me want to change my life. To . . .
participate. I know it's not possible and that you
have a boyfriend and we're not . . . compatible or
whatever but . . . I just . . . I know it's stupid . . . but   10
maybe just hear me out for a second and then you
can tell me I'm an idiot and we'll both go back in
and pretend this never happened but . . . I want to
travel the world with you. I want to bring the ice
cold **Amstel to your Greek shore**. And sit in silence   15
and sip with you. I want to go to Tesco's with you of
a Sunday. Watch you sleep, scrub your back, rub
your shoulders, suck your toes. I want to write crap
poetry about you, lay my coat over puddles for you,
always have a handkerchief available for you. I want   20
to get drunk and bore my friends about you, I want
them to phone up and moan about how little they
see me because I'm spending so much time with
you. I want to feel the tingle of our lips meeting,
the lock of our eyes joining, the fizz of our   25
fingertips touching. I want to touch your fat tummy
and tell you you look gorgeous in maternity
dresses, I want to stand next to you wide-eyed and
hold my nose as we open that first used nappy, I

Amstel to your Greek shore earlier in the play Ruth said that her ideal place was a
beach on a Greek island, with a bottle of Amstel wine.

want to watch you grow old and love you more and more each day. I want to fall in love with you.
I think I could. And I think it would be good.
And I want you to say yes. You might feel the
same.

Beat.

Could you? Maybe?

---

2 Write down or discuss a few words which sum up Tony's mood.
Nervous, passionate, thrilled or desperate might be possibilities.
Angry, indifferent or sulky are probably not.

3 Choose an intention for Tony. Here are some suggestions, although
you may have a different idea of your own:

- to persuade
- to charm
- to explain
- to seduce
- to grab life by the collar.

Try some different intentions and see which you think works best.
(As an experiment, try a couple that you do not think are
appropriate as well, for example to bully or to repel.)

4 Reread Constance's speech or Edmund's speech in A4: Connecting
(pages 16 and 17 respectively). What intention or intentions do you
think work for those?

Choosing an intention for what a character is saying will improve your
performance by adding clarity and depth.

A6: Interacting

This chapter explores how to establish relationships between
characters and how to communicate these clearly to the audience.

The short ***duologues*** which follow (pages 23–9) are taken from plays written in two languages over a period of five centuries (a duologue is a piece spoken by two actors). They are very different but, regardless of when and where the play was written and the language the characters use, the first task is to read the text for clues about who the characters are and what is happening in the scene.

1 Working with a partner, choose one duologue to work on. Read the scene aloud twice – once in each role – before deciding who will play whom.

2 With your partner, make notes about, or discuss, the following questions:

   - Do these characters know each other? How well?
   - If they do, how long is it since they last saw each other?
   - What do they feel about each other?
   - What do they want from each other?

   (At this stage, 'Don't know' or 'Can't tell' are acceptable answers!)

Writer: William Shakespeare
Country: England
Date: 1600
Characters: Beatrice and Benedick
Context: The play is set at the time it was written. Benedick has just returned from war. He and his companions have just arrived in the town where Beatrice lives with her uncle.

 Much Ado About Nothing

BEATRICE   I wonder that you will still be talking, Signor Benedick, nobody marks you.

BENEDICK   What, my dear Lady **Disdain**! Are you yet living?

Disdain contempt or scorn: Benedick is saying she is always sarcastic.

BEATRICE	Is it possible Disdain should die, while she hath such meet food to feed it, as Signor Benedick? 5 Courtesy itself must convert to Disdain, if you come in her presence.
BENEDICK	Then is Courtesy a **turn-coat**: but it is certain I am loved of all ladies, only you excepted: and I would I could find in my heart that I had 10 not a hard heart, for truly I love none.
BEATRICE	**A dear happiness to** women, they would else have been troubled with a **pernicious suitor**. I thank God and my cold blood, I am of your humour for that: I had rather hear my dog bark 15 at a crow than a man swear he loves me.
BENEDICK	God keep your ladyship still in that mind, so some gentleman or other shall **scape** a **predestinate** scratched face.
BEATRICE	Scratching could not make it worse, **and** 'twere 20 such a face as yours were.
BENEDICK	Well, you are a rare parrot-teacher.
BEATRICE	A bird of my tongue is better than a beast of yours.
BENEDICK	I would my horse had the speed of your tongue, 25 and **so good a continuer**: but keep your way **a** God's name. I have done.
BEATRICE	You always end with a **jade**'s trick: I know you of old.

---

turn-coat traitor; **A dear happiness to** a piece of good luck for.
pernicious suitor unpleasant potential husband; **scape** escape;
predestinate decided beforehand; **and** if;
so good a continuer so much staying power; **a** in; **jade** a nagging woman.

Writer: Noël Coward
Country: Great Britain
Date: 1941
Characters: Charles and Elvira
Context: The play is set at the time it was written. Charles, a writer, has arranged a séance; he does not believe in the supernatural – it is part of the research for his new book. During the séance, Elvira has returned from the dead. This is unfortunate, as Charles, her husband, is now married to Ruth.

 Blithe Spirit

CHARLES	This is obviously a hallucination, isn't it?
ELVIRA	I'm afraid I don't know the technical term for it.
CHARLES	What am I to do?
ELVIRA	What Ruth suggested – relax.
CHARLES	Where have you come from?
ELVIRA	Do you know, it's very peculiar, but I've sort of forgotten.
CHARLES	Are you here to stay indefinitely?
ELVIRA	I don't know that either.
CHARLES	Oh, my God!
ELVIRA	Why, would you hate it so much if I was?
CHARLES	Well, you must admit it would be embarrassing.
ELVIRA	I don't see why, really – it's all a question of adjusting yourself – anyhow I think it's horrid of you to be so unwelcoming and disagreeable.
CHARLES	Now look here, Elvira . . .
ELVIRA	I do – I think you're mean.

5

10

15

| CHARLES | Try to see my point, dear – I've been married to Ruth for five years, and you've been dead for seven . . . | 20 |

| ELVIRA | Not dead, Charles – 'passed over'. It's considered vulgar to say 'dead' where I come from. |

| CHARLES | Passed over, then. |

| ELVIRA | At any rate, now that I'm here, the least you can do is to make a pretence of being amiable about it . . . | 25 |

| CHARLES | Of course, my dear, I'm delighted in one way . . . |

| ELVIRA | I don't believe you love me any more. |

| CHARLES | I shall always love the memory of you. | 30 |

| ELVIRA | You mustn't think me unreasonable, but I really am a little hurt. You called me back – and at great inconvenience I came – and you've been thoroughly churlish ever since I arrived. |

| CHARLES | Believe me, Elvira, I most emphatically did not send for you – there's been some mistake. | 35 |

Writer: Wendy Kesselman
Country: United States of America
Date: 1980
Characters: Christine and Lea
Context: The play is set in France in the early 1930s. Christine and Lea are both maids in a house ruled with a rod of iron by Madame Danzard. (This is a very good play if you are looking for something with an all-female cast of four.)

 ## My Sister In This House

> *Christine goes upstairs into their room. Lea, hastily folding up the letter, looks at her guiltily.*

CHRISTINE	What is it, Lea? Another letter from **Maman**?
	Lea looks away.
	Well, go on. Read it. There's no reason to stop just because I came into the room. *(She takes off her long apron and folds it neatly.)*
LEA	I'll read it later.
CHRISTINE	You won't have time later. You're exhausted by ten. Read it now.
	Lea looks at her.
	Why don't you read it out loud?
LEA	*(nervously)* Do you really want me to?
CHRISTINE	I wouldn't say it otherwise, would I?
LEA	*(unfolding the letter, begins to read)* 'Lea, my pet, my little dove. I know I'll see you Sunday as usual, but I miss you. Little Lea. You'll always be little.'
	Lea looks anxiously at Christine.
CHRISTINE	Go on.
LEA	*(continuing)* 'Don't forget to bring me the money. You forgot last week.'
CHRISTINE	Poor Maman.
LEA	Christine – Maman just –
CHRISTINE	Maman just what? Go ahead. Keep reading.
LEA	*(going on with the letter)* 'You can't wear your hair that way anymore, Lea. Like a child. All that long hair.' *(She stops.)*
CHRISTINE	Well? Don't leave anything out.
LEA	*(going on)* 'Next Sunday, when you come, I'll fix it

Line numbers in right margin: 5 (at "ten. Read it now."), 10 (at "little dove"), 15 (at "You forgot last week."), 20 (at "that way anymore, Lea. Like a child. All that long")

Maman Mum.

for you. It'll be better that way. Like Christine's. Won't fall in the soup.' 25

Lea looks up, laughing. Christine doesn't smile. Going back to the letter. Quickly.

'Or get Christine to fix it for you. But tell her to be gentle.'

CHRISTINE	*(snatching the letter from Lea)* I'm never going back.
LEA	Christine.
CHRISTINE	*(folding the letter up very small)* You can go if you want to. 30
LEA	You know I wouldn't without you.
CHRISTINE	But you still care for her. She loves you.
LEA	But Christine, Christine. Maman loves you too. She's just . . . 35
CHRISTINE	What?
LEA	. . . scared of you.
CHRISTINE	Scared of me? *(giving the tiny folded up letter back to Lea)* You never stick up for me. But that's right. Defend her. Take her part. Like you always do. 40

Writer: Clifford Oliver
Country: Great Britain
Date: 1997
Characters: Kenny and Showab
Context: The play is set at the time it was written. Showab is the first Asian British premiere league football player. He has just been sent off.

 Ooh Ah Showab Khan

Showab enters, he is about twenty years old and wearing a muddy football kit. He is obviously upset and angry. He tears off his shirt and throws it at the wall.

He sits and buries his head in his hands.

Kenny enters. He is about forty. He is the team coach and is dressed in a track suit.

KENNY   Nice one.

He waits for a response – there is none.

No, if you're going to screw up, screw up big time.

SHOWAB   Yeah.

KENNY   Yeah. Well, it could have been worse. I mean, you 5 didn't actually leap the wall and 'Kung Fu' kick anyone in the crowd.

SHOWAB   Leave it.

KENNY   No, I'm not going to leave it. What's the matter with you? 10

SHOWAB   Nothing. *(He gets up, takes a towel from his bag and starts to walk off.)*

KENNY   Don't walk away from me. I might be the only friend you've got and believe me, after what you just did you're going to need friends.

Showab stops.

So what happened? 15

SHOWAB   I don't know. I just lost it.

KENNY   Yeah, you can say that again.

SHOWAB   Look, you weren't out there, you didn't have to take it.

KENNY   Ah, did the nasty man call you bad names? 20

SHOWAB   Yes, he did. And I don't have to take that crap.

KENNY   So you showed him.

SHOWAB   Yeah.

KENNY   And you got yourself sent off and he's still
out there. And we're a goal down at home, and   25
if we lose this the boss is going to put it down
to you.

Status – the position, rank or importance a person has in society – is a
fundamental concept in exploring the interaction between characters
in Drama.

3   To explore who has the power and status within the scene, you
and your partner should list as many status relationships as you
can think of. First think in general terms, for example:

- teacher and pupil
- football team captain and football player
- shop manager and part-time shop worker
- Prime Minister and Member of Parliament.

Next, use your own experience to make notes on the following
points:

- Who has higher status than you do?

- Who has lower status than you do?

- What gives someone status in a particular situation?

- Why might someone's status vary depending on the situation
  they are in?

Stand facing your scene partner, approximately five paces apart.
Read through the duologue and, as you speak each line, step
forward, step back or remain on the same spot, depending on
whether you feel that the character is gaining status, losing status
or maintaining the status quo (the existing relationship) at that
point in the scene. Pause to discuss your ideas and opinions with
your partner whenever necessary: you might not be sure what is
happening to the character, or you might disagree with your
partner's interpretation. That is fine.

- Record what you decide, paying particular attention to whether one character retains high or low status, whether the status is reversed during the scene or whether it moves backwards and forwards throughout the scene.

- Create two still pictures, one for the beginning and one for the end of the scene, which use body language, spatial relationships (i.e. how near or far the characters are from each other), levels, eye contact and gesture to communicate the relative status of the characters. Show the still pictures to the rest of the group and ask them to state what your pictures tell them about the relationship between the two characters.

If you have not communicated what you want, how will you change the picture to make it clearer?

4 Use the activity on intentions in A5: Communicating (Activity 3, page 22) to try out different intentions for each character. For instance, does your character want to charm, to upset, to ignore, to bully, to flatter, to defeat? Is the intention to inform, to question or to pass on information? How does the intention that underpins each speech change as the scene progresses?

Distillation means paring the scene down to capture, in whatever way you think best, the essence of the interaction between the characters.

5 To do this, rehearse and show a silent scene with your partner, based on the duologue on which you are working. It should not be a mime, but simply a scene where the body language, the spatial relationships, the eye contact (or lack of it) and physical contact create an atmosphere which captures what, for you and your partner, is important about the relationship between the two characters.

Show and discuss what has been communicated. If other pairs have been working on the same duologue, compare and contrast different interpretations.

6   Now develop this by adding ten words (in total, not each) to communicate the essence of the scene more clearly, based on what your audience has told you.

7   Use all that you have discovered in the previous activities to perform your interpretation of the scene. Revisit your answers to the questions in Activity 2 and see how your practical work has deepened your understanding of the relationship between the characters.

To improve your future work, make some notes that will help you interpret other characters and other scenes by answering the question:

• What are the different tools and exercises that actors can use to communicate relationships in a way that is clear to the audience?

A7: Beginnings

Chapters A7–A11 explore different techniques and conventions for building a play. These will help you analyse how playwrights structure plays, and they will also give you ideas on how to structure and develop your own devised work.

The aim of this chapter is to explore what makes an effective opening for a piece of theatre. Everyone has watched a play or video or film and decided within the first few minutes whether it has engaged their attention – whether to keep watching to find out what happens next.

1   What makes *you* want to watch a play? How much information – if any – do you need about what has happened before the play begins? With a partner, make notes or discuss a play or video or film you have seen where the opening made you want to keep watching. Why did it do so?

The first extract in this chapter is the opening scene from *The Alchemist*, a play written in 1610 by Ben Jonson. Face is a servant whose master, Lovewit, is away. Face has met Subtle and Dol Common, two beggars who live by their wits. The three rogues are using Lovewit's house as the base for their con operation. They are pretending that Subtle is an alchemist, who can turn base metal (the lowest of the three classes of metal) into gold. Foolish people flock to the house hoping to become very wealthy – for a price!

The Alchemist

Lovewit's house in Blackfriars. Enter Face, Subtle, and Dol Common.

FACE	Believe 't, I will.
SUBTLE	Thy worst. I fart at thee.
DOL	**Ha' you your wits?** Why gentlemen! For love –
FACE	**Sirrah**, I'll strip you –
SUBTLE	What to do? Lick figs Out at my –
FACE	Rogue, rogue, **out of all your sleights**.
DOL	Nay, look ye! Sovereign, General, are you mad-men? 5
SUBTLE	O, let the wild sheep loose. I'll gum your silks With **good strong water**, an' you come.
DOL	Will you have The neighbours hear you? Will you betray all? Hark, I hear some body.
FACE	Sirrah –

Ha' you your wits? Have you gone mad?; **Sirrah** mate;
out of all your sleights stop playing your tricks; **good strong water** acid.

SUBTLE	I shall **mar**
	All that the tailor has made, if you approach. 10
FACE	You most notorious **whelp**, you insolent slave.
	Dare you do this?
SUBTLE	Yes faith, yes faith.
FACE	Why! Who
	Am I, my mongrel? Who am I?
SUBTLE	I'll tell you,
	Since you know not your self –
FACE	Speak lower, rogue.
SUBTLE	Yes. You were once (time's not long past) the good, 15
	Honest, plain, **livery-three-pound-thrum**; that kept
	Your master's worship's house, here, in the **Friars**,
	For the vacations –
FACE	Will you be so loud?
SUBTLE	Since, by my means, **translated suburb-Captain**.
FACE	By your means, Doctor Dog?
SUBTLE	Within man's memory, 20
	All this, I speak of.
FACE	Why, I pray you, have I
	Been **countenanc'd** by you? Or you, by me?
	Do but **collect**, sir, where I met you first.
SUBTLE	I do not hear well.
FACE	Not of this, I think it.
	But I shall put you in mind, sir, at **Pie Corner**. 25

---

mar ruin; **whelp** puppy or cub;
livery-three-pound-thrum a badly paid (£3 per year) servant dressed in cheap
uniform;
Friars Blackfriars, the area of London where the play is set (and also the theatre
where it was first performed);
translated suburb-Captain turned into a pimp and con-man;
countenanc'd done a good turn; **collect** remember, recollect;
Pie Corner an area of cheap food stalls in Smithfield Market, in London.

Taking your meal of steam in, from cooks' stalls,
Where, like the father of hunger, you did walk
Piteously **costive**, with your **pinch'd-horn-nose**.

SUBTLE I wish, you could advance your voice, a little.

FACE **When you went pinn'd up, in the several rags,** 30
Yo' had rak'd, and pick'd from dung-hills, before
day,
Your feet in mouldy slippers, for your **kibes**,
A felt of rug, and a thin threaden cloak,
That scarce would cover your no-buttocks –

SUBTLE   So, sir!

FACE When all your **alchemy**, and your algebra, 35
Your minerals, vegetals, and animals,
Your conjuring, **coz'ning**, and your dozen of trades,
Could not relieve your corpse, with so much linen
Would make you **tinder**, but to see a fire;
I ga' you count'nance, credit for your coals, 40
Your stills, your glasses, your materials,
Built you a furnace, drew you customers,
Advanc'd all your black arts; lent you, beside,
A house to practise in –

SUBTLE   Your master's house!

FACE Where you have studied the more **thriving** skill 45
Of **bawdry**, since.

---

costive with an aching stomach;
pinch'd-horn-nose a nose like a shoe horn – thin with hunger;
When you went . . . dung hills, before day dressed in rags picked up from scrap
heaps; **kibes** chilblains;
alchemy magical process (fake in Subtle's case) for turning metal into gold;
coz'ning cheating; tinder small pieces of wood used to start a fire;
I ga' you count'nance . . . materials I took you in and advanced money for the
things you needed to pretend to be an alchemist; **thriving** profitable;
bawdry pimping and deceiving.

SUBTLE	Yes, in your master's house.
	You, and the rats, here, kept possession.
FACE	The place has made you **valiant**.
SUBTLE	No, your clothes.
	Thou vermin, have I ta'en thee, out of dung,
	So poor, so wretched, when no living thing $\quad$ 50
	Would keep thee company, but a spider, or worse?
	Rais'd thee from brooms, and dust, and wat'ring
	$\quad$ pots?
	Put thee in words, and fashion? Made thee fit
	For more than ordinary fellowships?
	Made thee a second, in mine own great art? $\quad$ 55
	And have I this for thank? Do you rebel?
	Do you fly out, i' the projection?
	Would you be gone, now?
DOL	Gentlemen, what mean you?
	Will you mar all?
SUBTLE	Slave, thou hadst had no name –
DOL	Will you undo your selves, with **civil war**? $\quad$ 60
FACE	Sirrah –
DOL	Nay, General, I thought you were **civil** –
FACE	I shall turn desperate, if you grow thus loud.
SUBTLE	And hang thy self, I care not.
FACE	Hang thee, **collier**,
	And all my pots, and pans, in picture I will,
	Since thou hast mov'd me. –
DOL	(O, this'll o'er-throw all.) 65

---

valiant brave;
Do you fly out, i' the projection? Do you explode at the final stage of the
alchemical process?; **civil war** fighting between ourselves; **civil** sensible;
collier a charcoal burner (i.e. a lowly job, so another insult).

SUBTLE	Away, you **trencher-rascal**.
FACE	Out you **dog-leach**,

FACE   Out you **dog-leach**,
The vomit of all prisons –

DOL   Will you be
Your own destructions, gentlemen?

FACE   Still spew'd out
For **lying too heavy o' the basket**.

SUBTLE   Cheater.

FACE   Bawd.

SUBTLE   Cow-herd.

FACE   Conjurer.

SUBTLE   **Cut-purse**.

FACE   Witch.

DOL   O, me!   70
We are ruin'd! Lost! Ha' you no more regard
To your reputations? Where's your judgement?
   'Slight,
Have yet, some care of me, o' your **republic** –

She catcheth out Face his sword: and breaks Subtle's glass.

And you, sir, with your **menstrue**, gather it up.
'Sdeath, you abominable pair of stinkards,   75
Leave off your barking, and grow one again,
Or, by the light that shines, I'll cut your throats.
I'll not be made a prey unto the **marshal**,
For ne'er a snarling **dog-bolt** o' you both.

---

trencher-rascal a lowly servant (i.e. an insult);
dog-leach a parasite on a dog (i.e an insult);
lying too heavy o' the basket eating more than his fair share of prison rations
(friends of prisoners brought in food in baskets);
Cut-purse pickpocket; **'Slight** an oath (God's light); **republic** joint interests;
menstrue a solvent used in alchemy; **'Sdeath** an oath (God's death); **marshal** police;
dog-bolt worthless person.

Ha' you together cozen'd all this while,   80
And all the world, and shall it now be said
Yo' have made most courteous shift, to cozen your
    selves?
(to Face) You will accuse him? You will **bring him in
Within the statute**? Who shall take your word?
A whore-son, upstart, **apocryphal** captain,   85
Whom not a puritan, in Blackfriars, will trust.
(to Subtle) You must be chief? As if you, only, had
The **powder** to project with? And the work
Were not begun out of equality?
The **venter tripartite**? All things in common?   90
Fall to your couples again, and cozen kindly,
Or, by this hand, I shall grow **factious** too,
And, take my part, and quit you.

FACE   'Tis his fault,
He ever murmurs, and objects his pains,
And says, the weight of all lies upon him.   95

SUBTLE Why, so it do's.

DOL   How does it? Do not we
Sustain our parts?

SUBTLE   Yes, but they are not equal.

DOL Why, if your part exceed to day, I hope
Ours may, to morrow, match it.

SUBTLE   Ay, they may.

DOL May, murmuring mastiff? Ay, and do. Death on me!   100
(to Face) Help me to throttle him.

---

bring him . . . statute report him to the police;
apocryphal pretend; **powder** i.e. powder ground from the philosopher's stone;
venter tripartite i.e. they began their business as three equal partners;
factious quarrelsome.

SUBTLE	**Dorothy**, Mistress Dorothy,
	'Ods precious, I'll do any thing. What do you mean?
DOL	Because o' your **fermentation**, and **cibation**?
SUBTLE	Not I, by heaven –
DOL	Your **Sol**, and **Luna** – *(to Face)* help me.
SUBTLE	Would I were hang'd then. I'll conform myself.	105
DOL	Will you, sir, do so then, and quickly: swear.
SUBTLE	What should I swear?
DOL	To **leave your faction**, sir.
	And labour, kindly, in the commune work.
SUBTLE	Let me not breathe, if I meant **aught**, beside.
	I only us'd those speeches, as a spur	110
	To him.
DOL	I hope we need no spurs, sir. Do we?
FACE	**'Slid**, prove to day, who shall **shark** best.
SUBTLE	Agreed.
DOL	Yes, and work close, and friendly.
	The door bell rings.
SUBTLE	Who's that? One rings. To the window, Dol. Pray heav'n,
	The master do not trouble us, this **quarter**.	115

Dorothy Dol is a nickname for Dorothy;
'Ods precious an oath (God's precious [blood]);
fermentation
cibation } two actions in the alchemical process;
Sol the sun
Luna the moon } two stages in the alchemical process;
leave your faction stop your quarrel; **aught** anything; **'Slid** an oath (God's
eyelids);
shark swindle, cheat; **quarter** three-month period.

FACE	O, fear not him. While there dies one a week,
	O' the plague, he's safe, from thinking toward
	London.
	Beside, he's busy at his hop-yards, now:
	I had a letter from him. If he do,
	He'll send such word, for airing o' the house 120
	As you shall have sufficient time, to quit it:
	Though we break up a fortnight, 'tis no matter.
SUBTLE	Who is it, Dol?
DOL	A fine young **quodling**.
FACE	O,
	My lawyer's clerk, I **lighted on**, last night,
	In Holborn, at the Dagger. He would have 125
	(I told you of him) a **familiar**,
	To **rifle** with, at horses, and win cups.
DOL	O, let him in.
SUBTLE	Stay. Who shall do 't?
FACE	**Get you**
	Your robes on. I will meet him, as going out.
DOL	And what shall I do?
FACE	Not be seen, away. 130

Exit Dol.

	Seem you very **reserv'd**.
SUBTLE	Enough.

Exit Subtle.

FACE	God b'w' you, sir.
	I pray you, let him know that I was here.
	His name is Dapper.

---

quodling unsophisticated youth;
lighted on met; **familiar** guardian angel; **rifle** gamble;
Get you . . . on put on your alchemist's costume; **reserv'd** shy.

2   Work in a group of three to rehearse and perform the scene.
    (Alternatively, you may wish to work in a group of four, with one
    of you assigned the role of director.) Read the scene once or
    twice. Before you begin rehearsing it, revisit these earlier
    activities:

    - A1: Moving, Activities 3 and 4 (pages 3–4), to help physicalise
      these bold, energetic characters and to use space effectively as
      their quarrel progresses
    - A2: Breathing, Activity 4 (page 13): there are some long
      speeches which need all the breath you can muster
    - A5: Communicating, Activity 3 (page 22), to establish their
      intentions
    - A6: Interacting, Activity 3 (page 30), to explore how status shifts
      within the scene.

The Alchemist is an example of a play that starts with a bang: the
characters burst on stage, cursing and fighting. The **exposition** –
which means providing the audience with any necessary information –
is part of the action. The quarrel between Subtle and Face, and Dol
Common's interjections, reveal how they all came to be in the same
place and what they are doing there.

Here are four more beginnings for you to analyse. Once again, the
extracts are deliberately chosen to show that, regardless of when and
where a play was written, there are certain questions that can and
should be asked by anyone performing or studying it.

Writer: William Shakespeare
Country: England
Date: c. 1605

Macbeth

Thunder and lightning. Enter Three Witches.

FIRST WITCH	When shall we three meet again?
	In thunder, lightning, or in rain?
SECOND WITCH	When the **hurlyburly**'s done
	When the battle's lost and won.
THIRD WITCH	That will be ere the set of sun. 5
FIRST WITCH	Where the place?
SECOND WITCH	Upon the heath.
THIRD WITCH	There to meet with Macbeth.
FIRST WITCH	I come, **Graymalkin**.
SECOND WITCH	**Paddock** calls.
THIRD WITCH	**Anon**!
ALL	Fair is foul, and foul is fair. 10
	Hover through the fog and filthy air.

---

hurlyburly confusion, turbulence (of the battle going on);
Graymalkin the witch's spirit attendant, a cat;
Paddock the witch's servant, a toad; **Anon** at once.

Writer: Agatha Christie
Country: Great Britain
Date: 1944

 ## And Then There Were None

Scene: The scene is the living room of the house on Indian Island. It is a very modern room, and luxuriously furnished. It is a bright sunlit evening. Nearly the whole of the back of the stage is a window looking directly out to sea. The French doors are wide so that a good area of the balcony is shown.

In the Left, near windows, is a door to dining room. Down stage Left is a door communicating with hall. Pull cord below this door.

Up Right is a door to study. Middle stage Right is fireplace. Over it hangs the reproduction of the 'Ten Little Indians' nursery rhyme. On the mantelpiece are a group of ten china Indian figures. They are not spaced out, but clustered so that the exact number is not easily seen.

*When Curtain rises, Rogers is busy putting final touches to room. He is setting out bottles down Right. Rogers is a competent middle-aged manservant. Not a butler, but a house-parlourman. Quick and deft. Just a trifle **specious** and shifty. There is a noise of seagulls. Motor boat horn heard off. Mrs Rogers enters from dining room up Left. She is a thin, worried, frightened-looking woman. Enter Narracott at Centre from Left. He carries a market basket filled with packages.*

NARRACOTT	First lot to be arriving in Jim's boat. Another lot not far behind. *(Crosses Left to her.)*
MRS ROGERS	Good evening, Fred.
NARRACOTT	Good evening, Mrs Rogers.
MRS ROGERS	Is that the boat?
NARRACOTT	Yes.
MRS ROGERS	Oh, dear, already? Have you remembered everything?
NARRACOTT	*(giving her basket)* I think so. Lemons. Slip soles. Cream. Eggs, tomatoes and butter. That's all, wasn't it?
MRS ROGERS	That's right. So much to do I don't know where to start. No maids till the morning, and all these guests arriving today.

5

10

specious pleasant expression, but deceptively so.

ROGERS	*(at mantel)* Calm down, Ethel, everything's shipshape now. Looks nice, don't it, Fred?	15
NARRACOTT	Looks neat enough to me. Kind of bare, but rich folks like places bare, it seems.	
MRS ROGERS	Rich folks is queer.	
NARRACOTT	And he was a queer sort of gentleman as built this place. Spent a wicked lot of money on it he did, and then gets tired of it and puts the whole thing up for sale.	20
MRS ROGERS	Beats me why the Owens wanted to buy it, living on an island.	25
ROGERS	Oh, come off it, Ethel, and take all that stuff out into the kitchen. They'll be here any minute now.	
MRS ROGERS	Making that steep climb an excuse for a drink, I suppose. Like some others I know.	30

Motor boat horn heard off.

| NARRACOTT | That be young Jim. I'll be getting along. |

Writer: Sam Shepard
Country: United States of America
Date: 1983

 ## Fool For Love

The Old Man sits in the rocker facing up right so he's just slightly profile to the audience. A bottle of whiskey sits on the floor beside him. He picks up bottle and pours whiskey into a styrofoam cup and drinks.

May sits on edge of bed facing audience, feet on floor, legs apart, elbows on knees, hands hanging limp and crossed between her knees, head hanging forward, face staring at floor. She is absolutely still and maintains this attitude until she speaks. She wears a blue denim full skirt, baggy white t-shirt and bare feet with a silver ankle bracelet. She's in her early thirties.

*Eddie sits in the upstage chair by the table, facing May. He wears muddy, broken-down cowboy boots with silver **gaffer's tape** wrapped around them at the toe and instep, well-worn, faded, dirty jeans that smell like horse sweat. Brown western shirt with **snaps**. A pair of spurs dangles from his belt. When he walks, he limps slightly and gives the impression he's rarely off a horse. There's a peculiar broken-down quality about his body in general, as though he's aged long before his time. He's in his late thirties.*

*On the floor, between his feet, is a leather bucking strap like **bronc** riders use. He wears a bucking glove on his right hand and works resin into the glove from a small white bag. He stares at May as he does this and ignores the Old Man.*

---

gaffer's tape wide, heavy-duty canvas-backed adhesive tape;
snaps fasteners, such as poppers; **bronc** a bronco is an untamed or half-tamed horse.

Writer: Molière
Country: France
Date: 1671

 Scapin the Schemer

Enter Octave and Sylvestre.

OCTAVE Could there be worse news for a suitor? My case is desperate indeed. You say, Sylvestre, you have just heard at the harbour that my father is coming home?

SYLVESTRE	Yes, Sir.	5

OCTAVE   He is expected to arrive this morning?

SYLVESTRE   This very morning.

OCTAVE   And he comes for the purpose of finding me a wife?

SYLVESTRE   Yes, Sir.   10

OCTAVE   A daughter of Seigneur Géronte?

SYLVESTRE   A daughter of Seigneur Géronte.

OCTAVE   That the girl has been sent for from Taranto?

SYLVESTRE   Yes.

OCTAVE   And you heard all this news from my uncle?   15

SYLVESTRE   From your uncle.

OCTAVE   Who had it from my father in a letter?

SYLVESTRE   In a letter.

OCTAVE   And my uncle knows all about our affairs?

SYLVESTRE   All about our affairs.   20

OCTAVE   Oh, for Heaven's sake, tell me everything straight out. Don't make me drag it out of you one word at a time.

SYLVESTRE   What more is there to say? You've described the situation quite correctly. You haven't   25
forgotten a thing.

OCTAVE   Well, give me some advice then. Tell me what I am to do, in the difficult position in which I find myself.

SYLVESTRE   Upon my word, I'm as much at a loss as you   30
are. I have as much need of advice myself.

OCTAVE   His coming home now has completely ruined me.

SYLVESTRE   Me too.

| OCTAVE | When my father hears what I have done, I shall have a regular storm of reproaches showering about my ears. | 35 |

| SYLVESTRE | Reproaches break no bones. I would to God I could get off so cheaply! But it looks as if I should have to pay a bit dearer for your foolery. I think I see a gathering storm of blows ready to burst on my shoulders. | 40 |

| OCTAVE | How the hell am I to get out of this mess? | |

| SYLVESTRE | You should have thought of that before you got into it. | 45 |

| OCTAVE | Oh, you make me sick with your ill-timed moralising. | |

| SYLVESTRE | You make me far sicker with your mad goings on. | |

| OCTAVE | But what now? What am I do to? Where is there a way out? | 50 |

---

3 With a partner, choose one of the extracts above and write one or two sentences in answer to each of the questions below.

Begin each sentence with the words 'I know . . .', if there is evidence in the text to support your answer, and quote the evidence from the text to back it up. Make it clear whether you are told (by a character speaking) or shown (by the location or the action of the scene).

If you are speculating, because there is nothing to tell you or because you are developing the evidence that is there, then begin with the words 'I think . . .'.

• Who are the characters (age, occupation, gender, social class)? Do they know each other? What is their attitude to each other?

- Where are they? How is this location conveyed (in stage directions, or in a character's speech)?
- What time is it? What has just happened? What will happen next?
- When and where is the play set? Can you tell this from the information contained in the text?
- When was it written? Could you tell this if the information had not already been provided?

4   What do your answers tell you about theatre at the place and time the play was written? For instance, if the writer does it all with words, what does that suggest about how the play was originally staged?

Some beginnings provide information. Sometimes, a writer does not begin with words but begins in silence, with an image or with action. Sometimes a beginning raises questions rather than answers them. There is no single right way to begin a play – engaging the audience's attention is what counts. Use what you have discovered in this chapter when you are devising your own scenes and plays, to help create an effective opening. Use it to help you analyse and understand the plays that you act, read or see on theatre trips as well.

A8: Narrating and Commentating

This chapter explores the different forms of **direct address**, which is when an actor speaks to the audience.

If the actor is acknowledging the audience by speaking to them, then the play is not naturalistic or realistic because, in real life, people do not step forward and address an audience. The **fourth wall** is the convention whereby actors pretend that there is no audience present and the audience imagines there is an invisible fourth wall between them and the performance. Film and television drama is almost always based on this convention – in fact, the screen provides the fourth wall. Nowadays we are used to this, but in fact **realism** and **naturalism** began as a reaction against the heightened, artificial style of nineteenth century drama. In Section B, you will learn more about the conventions of different forms of theatre.

1   Look through the earlier chapters of this book and decide which extracts involve direct address and in which there is a fourth wall.

The next extract is from the oldest European play still in existence, *The Oresteia*, written by Aeschylus and first performed in Greece in 456 BC. Greek tragedies such as *The Oresteia* introduced the idea of the **chorus**, a group of people who stand aside from the main action of the play and comment on it as well as describing events which have occurred or which we do not see. You will notice that none of the lines in the extract have been assigned to individual speakers. This is because the chorus was a group of actors. The chorus leader spoke individually, the rest of the chorus in unison. Sometimes lines may have been split between sections or single members of the chorus.

The extract is from a translation made by Ted Hughes in 1999. In it, the members of the chorus are elderly citizens of Athens, who have been waiting many years for their king, Agamemnon, to return from the Trojan Wars.

 ## The Oresteia

CHORUS   Let nobody tell you
          Heaven ignores
          The **desecrator**
          Who mocks and defiles
          The holy things –   5

          For they are wrong.
          Everywhere
          The conceited man
          With his lofty scheme

---

desecrator one who treats a holy place or object as not holy.

Ruins himself 10
And everybody near him.

The house where wealth
Cracks the foundations
With its sheer weight
Is a prison 15
Whose owner dies
In solitary.

What is enough?
Who knows? Once
A man in the **stupor** 20
Of wealth and pride
Has broken heaven's law
And kicked over
The altar of justice
It is too late. 25

Voluptuous promises,
Crystalline logic,
Caressing assurances
Lead him, the slave
Of his own destruction. 30

. . .

Running after pleasure,
Thoughtless, careless
As a boy
Chasing a bird.
He ruins his people. 35
He prays, but the gods
Are bedrock rock.
And men who pity him
Share his fate.

---

stupor lack of awareness;
Crystalline like crystal (beautiful but with a complicated structure).

So **Paris** came,   40
Light-hearted, a guest
Honoured at the table
Of **Menelaus** –
And in contempt
Of the **house of Atreus**   45
And heaven's law
Stole his host's wife.

The light-footed Helen
Flitted with Paris.
She left in Argos   50
A thunder of anger,
Hammering of bronze,
Assembling of ships,
And took to Troy
Her terrible dowry –   55
Annihilation.

Menelaus went mad.
He lay on their bed –
A man in a trance.
His soul fluttered   60
Above the **Aegean**.
Sleeping, he shouted –
Tortured by dreams.
She was running away
With laughing Paris.   65
She lay there, laughing
With laughing Paris.
King Menelaus

Paris a Trojan prince;
Menelaus Paris' host and Helen's husband, King of Argos;
house of Atreus the family or tribe of Menelaus and Agamemnon, his brother;
Aegean the Aegean Sea.

Cried through the nights
Like a lost child.   70

And woke to be tortured
By her statue –
Her painted eyes
That stared at him
From a stone body.   75

So much for the grief of our greatest house.
But he who sailed for Troy with all our men
Left a grief behind him that crushed Argos –
The men who had gone with him began to come
    back.

They came back   80
To widows,
To fatherless children,
To screams, to sobbing.
The men came back
As **little clay jars**   85
Full of sharp cinders.

War is a pawnbroker – not of your treasures
But of the lives of your men. Not of gold but of
    corpses.
Give your man to the war-god and you get ashes.
Your hero's exact worth – in the coinage of war.   90

Such a great hero – he made just this much **slag**.
Then the widows weep face-eating acid.
The house of Atreus has ruined their houses.
The King cashed in their men – and bought a
    whore.

---

little clay jars . . . **cinders** i.e. dead (cremated);
slag refuse matter separated from the metal of the coinage i.e. 'a great hero' was, in
the coinage of war, worthless.

The gusty wind   95
On the plains of Troy
Has torn the voices
Out of their chests
And scattered like smoke
The shapes of their faces   100
And puffed them inland
To cool Helen.

Now throughout Argos
The mourning for the slain
Gathers like a curse.   105
Rulers should fear,
Above all, one thing:
The gathering curse
Of their own people.

It curdles the daylight   110
Thick as a darkness –
A fear in the air.
A weight you can feel
And have to bear.

That leader who herds   115
His people en masse
Into glorious graves –
Let him be sure:
Heaven is watching.
When his high hand   120
Unbalances justice
The Furies wake up.
That man strides
Assured and proud
Into the **abyss**.   125

The Furies in Greek mythology, three women who avenge crimes;
abyss bottomless pit.

2 Discuss and decide:
   - What information (exposition) does the chorus provide for the audience?
   - What is their attitude to the events they describe?
   - Why could they not show the events described?

Greek tragedy was originally performed in huge outdoor amphitheatres. This led to a particular style of performance. The acoustics were perfect, which meant that an actor could use great vocal variety and be heard. But the size of the auditorium meant that facial expressions would have been invisible to the middle of the audience, let alone to the back row. For that reason, all actors wore large masks made of light wood, cork or linen: these masks showed the age and sex of the character portrayed, and also displayed any dominant characteristic emotions such as fear, rage, jealousy, greed. Because of the size of the theatre, larger than life gestures were also necessary.

3 Work in a group of five. Choose a short extract (maximum 20 lines) from *The Oresteia* and stage that extract using the conventions of Greek theatre:
   - large gestures, which match the emotion or mood of each line
   - masks
   - some lines spoken in unison, some lines spoken by individuals.

Shakespeare also used the idea of the chorus, but concentrated the function in a single person. Sometimes, in plays like *Romeo and Juliet,* the Chorus is named as such, and introduces the play. Sometimes a character takes on the function of the chorus, stepping in and out of the action. Puck, in *A Midsummer Night's Dream,* is one such character, as is the Bastard in *King John*.

4 Analyse a Shakespeare play that you have read or seen. Discuss and decide if there is a character who steps out of the action to comment on it.

There are many examples of the chorus in twentieth-century Drama. The following extract comes from Olwen Wymark's 1987 dramatisation of *Nana*, the nineteenth-century novel by Emile Zola. The extract takes place at the Théâtre des Variétés in Paris in 1868. Nana is a young woman who fights her way out of the slums by becoming an actress, and then a courtesan (a high-class prostitute), who becomes the toast of Parisian high society.

 Nana

At the sound of the overture all the actors go swiftly and excitedly to sit in the chairs. They are now not specific characters but members of the audience of the Théâtre des Variétés. They talk animatedly to each other, calling over their shoulders, laughing, shouting, sometimes standing up etc.

1: It's all about the gods, this operetta.

2: What a crowd. The place is packed!

3: Who's ever heard of Nana?

4: Posters plastered all over town.

5: She comes from the slums, this Nana.   5

6: Who wrote the music?

7: Bordenave's spent a fortune.

8: Her father was a drunken builder.

9: Her mother was a cheap whore.

10: It's so hot!   10

11: All the critics in Paris are here.

12: Nana's going to be a hit!

13: She'll be a disaster. Never acted in her life.

14: She's playing Venus.

15: Nana! The Goddess of Love!   15

16: Blonde and buxom.

17: She's sensational!

18: A ball of fire!

19: Nana Nana!

20: *(All)* Let's see Venus! We want Nana! Nana! Nana! Nana! 20

There is a loud chord and they all get up immediately and flourishing the chairs in the air and shouting Nana's name they go off to the dressing room areas. Now they are the performers in the operetta. There is much movement and bustle between the two dressing rooms as they get into their costumes and bring on the set pieces for the operetta. These consist of a big cut out shell upstage centre (behind which is the actress playing Nana) and some cut out waves. During all this the actors speak the following:

1: Where's my **trident**?

2: Powder my back will you, Mathilde?

3: Move Fanton, you're in my way.

4: About time I had my own bloody dressing room. 25

5: Give us a drop of your brandy, Bosc.

6: Could somebody else have a look in the mirror Simonne?

7: Have you looked out front? It's a huge house.

8: Remember Gerard, we're taking the last exit much slower. 30

9: They're playing it far too fast.

10: I need a pin. Have you got a pin, Rose?

11: No!

---

trident a three-pronged spear (such as is carried by Neptune).

12: Here, I'll do it.   35

13: Have they called beginners yet?

14: Bags of time. Bags of time.

15: It has to be tighter.

16: If you have it that tight, you'll faint.

17: Will you tell them I need that in the wings for the   40
quick change?

18: Full company on stage. On stage ladies and
gentlemen, please.

19: God, I'm sweating like a pig in this costume.

20: Good luck, darling.   45

21: You too.

22: On stage, please!

---

5   Stage the scene from *Nana* in a group of four. You will need to
decide who speaks which line. You will notice that the playwright
uses transformation as a principle, so refer back to your work on
Bouncers in A1: Moving (pages 4–10), about how to provide
physicalisation for the characters and for ways of staging the
scene.

Here are a few more examples of plays that feature a chorus or a
character that fulfils that function:

- *Oedipus Rex* by Sophocles (c. 429 BC)
- *Henry V* by Shakespeare (c. 1598–9)
- *Antigone* by Jean Anouilh (1944)
- *The Glass Menagerie* by Tennessee Williams (1948)
- *The Life and Adventures of Nicholas Nickleby* by Charles Dickens
  (1839), dramatised by David Edgar (1979)
- *Dancing at Lughnasa* by Brian Friel (1990).

6 Choose one of the plays above (or find another play which features a chorus) and answer the following questions:

- Does the chorus have a character name?
- Does the chorus sometimes take part in the action of the play, or are they always apart from the action?
- Does the chorus describe the world of the play and set the scene?
- Does the chorus have an attitude to the events of the play or characters in the play? If so, what?

To summarise, the chorus has a dual function: to narrate (either what has happened before the play or to recap what the audience has seen so far) and to comment on the action (to provide an attitude and help the audience know what to think or feel about the action of the play).

7 Show what you have learned about the chorus by working in groups to devise a scene which features a chorus which comments on the action.

A9: Revealing

This chapter explores various devices and conventions with which to express things which a character cannot or will not say to other characters.

The **soliloquy** is very like the convention of voiceover or 'spoken thoughts' which you have probably used in your own devised work. A soliloquy is a solo speech of some length, performed by a character as part of the play. The character is usually alone on the stage. However, a lone speaker on stage is not necessarily speaking a soliloquy. The Prologue to *Romeo and Juliet* is an example of a solo speech addressed to the audience. A long speech may be, but is not necessarily, a soliloquy either. The extract from *King John* (page 16) is not a soliloquy because in the play

Constance is talking to other characters on stage who hear and respond to her.

The soliloquy is a convention most used in sixteenth and seventeenth-century drama which enables a playwright to tell the audience what is going through a particular character's head. Characters speak their thoughts aloud because there is no one in the play that they can trust with these thoughts, or share them with. Of course, in real life, people do not stop and speak aloud all that is going through their heads, so the soliloquy is not a naturalistic convention. But, as with any convention, the audience can and does accept that this is what is happening.

1　Find an example of a soliloquy in one of Shakespeare's plays and discuss and decide what and why the character cannot share with others on stage.

The **aside**, where a character speaks their thoughts aloud, is another convention which is used a lot in Elizabethan and Jacobean theatre. There are two differences between the soliloquy and the aside

- the aside is only a line or two
- the aside is spoken when there are other characters on stage; in fact, it is called an aside because it is aside from the main dialogue.

The next extract is from *The Changeling* by Thomas Middleton and William Rowley, and was written in 1622. Beatrice is the spoilt daughter of a nobleman. De Flores is her father's servant and is so in love with Beatrice that he will find any excuse to see her. Beatrice hates him but now she needs his help. Her father has decided she should marry a wealthy nobleman but she loves another. She cannot defy her father. If only she could persuade someone to get rid of her fiancé, Alonzo. The extract begins with Beatrice trying to persuade herself to conceal her true feelings, as she waits for De Flores to arrive after she has summoned him.

The Changeling

BEATRICE	*(aside)* Why, because I loath'd him

BEATRICE *(aside)* Why, because I loath'd him
As much as youth and beauty hates a **sepulchre**,
Must I needs show it? Cannot I keep that secret,
And serve my turn upon him? – See, he's here.
– De Flores.

DE FLORES *(aside)* Ha, I shall run mad with joy,   5
She call'd me fairly by my name De Flores,
And neither rogue nor rascal.

BEATRICE What ha' you done to your face
A-late? Y'ave met with some good physician,
Y'ave prun'd your self me thinks, you were not
    wont   10
To look so amorously.

DE FLORES *(aside)*   Not I, 'tis
The same **physnomy** to a hair and pimple,
Which she call'd **scurvy** scarce an hour ago:
How is this?

BEATRICE   Come hither, nearer, man.

DE FLORES *(aside)* I'm up to the chin in heaven.

BEATRICE   Turn, let me see, 15
Vauh! 'tis but the heat of the liver, I perceiv't.
I thought it had been worse.

DE FLORES *(aside)*   Her fingers toucht me,
She smells all amber.

BEATRICE I'll make a water for you shall cleanse this
Within a fortnight.

DE FLORES   With your own hands, Lady? 20

---

sepulchre a tomb; **physnomy** i.e. physiognomy (face);
scurvy worthless, contemptible.

| BEATRICE | Yes, mine own sir; in a work of cure, |
| | I'll trust no other. |

| DE FLORES | *(aside)*   'Tis half an act of pleasure |
| | To hear her talk thus to me. |

| BEATRICE | We shall try you – |
| | Oh my De Flores! |

DE FLORES	*(aside)* How's that?
	She calls me hers already, my De Flores. 25
	– You were about to sigh out somewhat, Madam.

| BEATRICE | No, was I? I forgot – Oh! |

| DE FLORES | There 'tis again – |
| | The **very fellow on't**. |

| BEATRICE | You are too quick, sir. |

DE FLORES	There's no excuse for't, now I heard it twice,
	Madam, that sigh would **fain** have utterance, 30
	Take pity on't, and lend it a free word;
	'Las how it labours
	For liberty, I hear the murmur yet
	Beat at your bosom.

| BEATRICE | Would Creation – |

| DE FLORES | Ay, well said, that's it. |

| BEATRICE | – Had form'd me man.   35 |

| DE FLORES | Nay, that's not it. |

BEATRICE	Oh 'tis the soul of freedom,
	I should not then be forc'd to marry one
	I hate beyond all depths, I should have power
	Then to oppose my loathings, nay remove 'em
	For ever from my sight.

---

very fellow on't another sigh (i.e. he comments on her sigh again);
fain like to, wish to; **'Las** alas.

DE FLORES	*(aside)* Oh blest occasion!	40
	– Without change to your sex, you have your	
	wishes.	
	Claim so much man in me.	
BEATRICE	In thee De Flores? There's small cause for that.	
DE FLORES	Put it not from me, it's a service that	
	I kneel for to you. *(Kneels.)*	45
BEATRICE	You are too violent to mean faithfully,	
	There's horror in my service, blood and danger,	
	Can those be things to **sue for**?	
DE FLORES	If you knew	
	How sweet it were to me to be employed	
	In any act of yours, you would say then	50
	I fail'd, and use not reverence enough	
	When I receive the charge on't.	
BEATRICE	*(aside)* This is much methinks,	
	Belike his wants are greedy, and to such	
	Gold tastes like angels' food. – Rise.	
DE FLORES	**I'll have the work first**.	
BEATRICE	*(aside)* Possible his need	55
	Is strong upon him; *(gives him money)* – there's to	
	encourage thee:	
	As thou art **forward** and thy service dangerous,	
	Thy reward shall be precious.	
DE FLORES	That I have thought on,	
	I have assur'd my self of that beforehand,	
	And know it will be precious, the thought	
	ravishes.	60
BEATRICE	Then take him to thy fury.	

---

sue for to ask for;
I'll have the work first Tell me what the task is first;
forward co-operative; **ravishes** pleases and excites.

DE FLORES	I thirst for him.
BEATRICE	Alonzo de Piracquo.
DE FLORES	His **end**'s upon him,
	He shall be seen no more.
BEATRICE	How lovely now
	Dost thou appear to me! Never was man
	Dearlier rewarded.
DE FLORES	I do think of that. 65

---

end death.

The following activities will help you to stage the scene in such a way that you make it clear that the audience can hear what the character is saying as an aside, while the other character doesn't hear the words.

2 With a partner, discuss the following questions:

- Who has the higher status at the beginning of the scene?
- Does that character retain the higher status or does it change?

Ensure you know when the character is speaking to the other character and when speaking aside. (If it is not clear to you, the actor, how can it be clear to the audience?)

3 Try different ways of staging the scene so that the convention is clear to the audience. For instance:

- the other character could freeze
- the other characters could find some business with which to occupy themselves, so that the audience believes that they can't hear their words
- the character speaking their thoughts could acknowledge the audience – and perhaps try to enlist the audience's sympathy – or they could speak as if to themselves.

4 Use the following format to make notes on what the asides reveal about the characters:

  - De Flores thinks Beatrice thinks _____ about him. In fact she thinks _____.
  - Beatrice thinks De Flores will do what she wants because he wants _____. In fact he wants _____.

5 Use the convention of the aside to create a scene of your own, involving two people, where one is trying to ensnare or persuade the other and where both speak in asides to the audience.

6 Asides are also used in seventeenth and eighteenth century comedy, such as *The Rivals* (see pages 95–117) . As an alternative to *The Changeling*, stage an extract from *The Rivals* using the activities above.

Sub-text means what lies below (hence 'sub') the words that are spoken: sub-text therefore means what is not said. The soliloquy and the aside are conventions used in non-naturalistic theatre as a way of letting the audience know what a character is thinking but cannot say. In naturalistic drama, people do not stop the action and speak their thoughts aloud. So sub-text is the naturalistic equivalent of the soliloquy or the aside.

7 Words are just one form of communication. List all the other ways that you can think of in which communication occurs. These ways are known as non-verbal communication.

8 Think about a time when you could not say what you wanted to. Describe the situation. What did you want to say? What did you actually say? Why? Was it because you were embarrassed, or ashamed, or frightened, or didn't want to upset the other person or couldn't think quickly enough to work out what you wanted to say?

The following extract is the opening of *Far Away*, a play by Caryl Churchill written in 1999. Joan is a young girl and Harper is her aunt.

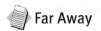 **Far Away**

Harper's house. Night.

JOAN	I can't sleep.
HARPER	It's the strange bed.
JOAN	No, I like different places.
HARPER	Are you cold?
JOAN	No.

5

HARPER	Do you want a drink?
JOAN	I think I am cold.
HARPER	That's easy enough then. There's extra blankets in the cupboard.
JOAN	Is it late?

10

HARPER	Two.
JOAN	Are you going to bed?
HARPER	Do you want a hot drink?
JOAN	No thank you.
HARPER	I should go to bed then.

· 15

JOAN	Yes.
HARPER	It's always odd in a new place. When you've been here a week you'll look back at tonight and it won't seem the same at all.
JOAN	I've been to a lot of places. I've stayed with friends at their houses. I don't miss my parents if you think that.

20

HARPER	Do you miss your dog?
JOAN	I miss the cat I think.
HARPER	Does it sleep on your bed?

25

JOAN	No because I chase it off. But it gets in if the door's not properly shut. You think you've shut

---

the door but it hasn't caught and she pushes it
open in the night.

HARPER Come here a minute. You're shivering. Are you hot? 30

JOAN No, I'm all right.

HARPER You're over-tired. Go to bed. I'm going to bed
myself.

JOAN I went out.

HARPER When? Just now? 35

JOAN Just now.

HARPER No wonder you're cold. It's hot in the daytime
here but it's cold at night.

JOAN The stars are brighter here than at home.

HARPER It's because there's no street lights. 40

JOAN I couldn't see much.

HARPER I don't expect you could. How did you get out?
I didn't hear the door.

JOAN I went out the window.

HARPER I'm not sure I like that. 45

JOAN No it's quite safe, there's a roof and a tree.

HARPER When people go to bed they should stay in bed.
Do you climb out of the window at home?

JOAN I can't at home because – No I don't.

HARPER I'm responsible for you. 50

JOAN Yes, I'm sorry.

HARPER Well that's enough adventures for one night.
You'll sleep now. Off you go. Look at you, you're
asleep on your feet.

JOAN There was a reason. 55

HARPER For going out?

JOAN I heard a noise.

HARPER An owl?

JOAN A shriek.

HARPER An owl then. There are all sorts of birds here, you might see a golden oriole. People come here specially to watch birds and we sometimes make tea or coffee or sell bottles of water because there's no café and people don't expect that and they get thirsty. You'll see in the morning what a beautiful place it is.

JOAN It was more like a person screaming.

HARPER It is like a person screaming when you hear an owl.

JOAN It was a person screaming.

HARPER Poor girl, what a fright you must have had imagining you heard somebody screaming. You should have come straight down here to me.

JOAN I wanted to see.

HARPER It was dark.

JOAN Yes but I did see.

HARPER Now what did you imagine you saw in the dark?

JOAN I saw my uncle.

HARPER Yes I expect you did. He likes a breath of air. He wasn't screaming I hope?

JOAN No.

HARPER That's all right then. Did you talk to him? I expect you were frightened he'd say what are you doing out of your bed so late.

JOAN I stayed in the tree.

HARPER He didn't see you?

JOAN No.

HARPER He'll be surprised won't he, he'll laugh when he hears you were up in the tree. He'll be cross but

	he doesn't mean it, he'll think it's a good joke, it's the sort of thing he did when he was a boy. So bed now. I'll go up too.
JOAN	He was pushing someone. He was bundling someone into a shed.
HARPER	He must have been putting a big sack in the shed. He works too late.
JOAN	I'm not sure if it was a woman. It could have been a young man.
HARPER	Well I have to tell you, when you've been married as long as I have. There are things people get up to, it's natural, it's nothing bad, that's just friends of his your uncle was having a little party with.
JOAN	Was it a party?
HARPER	Just a little party.
JOAN	Yes because there wasn't just that one person.
HARPER	No, there'd be a few of his friends.
JOAN	There was a lorry.
HARPER	Yes, I expect there was.
JOAN	When I put my ear against the side of the lorry I heard crying inside.
HARPER	How could you do that from up in the tree?
JOAN	I got down from the tree. I went to the lorry after I looked in the window of the shed.
HARPER	There might be things that are not your business when you're a visitor in someone else's house.
JOAN	Yes, I'd rather not have seen. I'm sorry.
HARPER	Nobody saw you?
JOAN	They were thinking about themselves.
HARPER	I think it's lucky nobody saw you.
JOAN	If it's a party, why was there so much blood?

Line numbers in right margin: 90, 95, 100, 105, 110, 115

9 Summarise the scene's plot in a single sentence.

10 With your partner from Activity 2, decide how much each character knows about whatever it is the uncle is doing. There are several possible interpretations and combinations of these interpretations, for example:

- the aunt is her husband's partner in crime
- the aunt is trying to find out how much the girl has seen
- the aunt has no idea what her husband is doing
- the girl is asking innocent questions
- the girl is suspicious.

You can probably think of several more.

11 Choose an intention (see A5: Communicating, pages 19–22) for each character to play. For example, Joan's intention might be 'to probe' while her aunt's might be 'to interrogate' (that is, find out how much Joan knows). With the relevant intention in mind, speak each character's thoughts aloud before every line that she speaks. For example:

> **JOAN** *There's something I want to ask you about but I don't know how.* I went out.
>
> **HARPER** *What does she know? What did she see?* When? Just now?

Be aware of the difference in tone, if any, between the spoken sub-text and the actual speech.

12 Decide which interpretation works best. Then stage a version of the scene without speaking the thoughts aloud, but using all you listed about non-verbal communication in Activity 7 to make the sub-text clear to the audience.

To summarise, a sub-text is made clear to the audience because the actors know what the sub-text is. They know because they have explored and experimented and decided as part of the rehearsal process. Often, when making and devising Drama, people say too much – too much information is conveyed by speech. When you are next devising a scene, try imposing a maximum number of words, as in the distillation activity in A6: Interacting (Activity 6, page 32) using instead all the other means of non-verbal communication.

A10: Building

This chapter looks at different ways of building the action – or plot – of a play. It will give you insight into and ideas about how to create and sustain **dramatic tension** (suspense) and how to maintain the audience's interest.

The next extract uses an age-old but very effective principle known as **dramatic irony**. This means that the audience knows more than most of the characters do.

This is the opening of *Rope* by Patrick Hamilton, first performed in 1929.

At the start of the play, the audience sees two characters bending over a chest and working at something. This creates dramatic tension because from the very beginning of the play the audience is asking, 'What has happened?' and then almost immediately, 'When and how will the murder be revealed?' As you read the scene, note how the fact that much of the scene takes place in darkness, and that the characters whisper, heightens the tense atmosphere.

 Rope

> *Curtain rises on room completely darkened save for the pallid gleam from lamplight in the street below, which comes through the window. Against this are silhouetted the figures of Granillo and Brandon. They are bending over the chest, intent, working at something – exactly what you cannot discern. The silence is complete. Suddenly the lid of the chest falls with a bang. Brandon goes over to window and draws the heavy curtains to. Complete black out. They*

continue whatever they are doing. Brandon murmurs 'All right, all right,' but there are no other sounds. Pause. Brandon comes down Right, and switches on the light at the little table.

GRANILLO *(at chest)* Put out that light! Put out that light!

Instantly it goes out.

BRANDON *(voice from darkness)* Steady, Granno.

No reply from other. Brandon is down right. Granillo is somewhere centre. Pause. Brandon suddenly lights a match and applies it to his cigarette. The cigarette glows in the darkness. He is now seated in the armchair. Pause.

BRANDON Feeling yourself, Granno?

No answer.

Feeling yourself again, Granno?

No answer.

Granno.   5

GRANILLO Give me some matches.

BRANDON Matches? Here you are. Coming.

He throws the matches over. They can be heard rattling in the air and falling on the floor. Granillo picks them up and lights his own cigarette. The two pin-points of light are all that come from the darkness. Pause.

It's about time you pulled yourself together, isn't it, Granno?

Pause.

GRANILLO You fully understand, Brandon, what we've done?   10

BRANDON	Do I know what I've done? . . . Yes. I know quite well what I've done. I have done murder.
GRANILLO	Yes.
BRANDON	I have committed murder. I have committed passionless – motiveless – faultless – and clueless murder. Bloodless and noiseless murder.
GRANILLO	Yes.
BRANDON	An **immaculate** murder. I have killed. I have killed for the sake of danger and for the sake of killing. And I am alive. Truly and wonderfully alive. That is what I have done, Granno. *(Long pause.)* What's the matter? Are you getting superstitious?
GRANILLO	No. I'm not superstitious.
BRANDON	*(suavely)* Then I may put on the light?
GRANILLO	No. You mayn't . . .

Their figures may now be dimly discerned in the faint glow from the fire.

Brandon?

BRANDON	Yes?
GRANILLO	You remember when Ronald came in? . . .
BRANDON	What do you mean – 'when Ronald came in'?
GRANILLO	When Ronald came in here . . . when he came in from the car. You were standing at the door.
BRANDON	Yes.
GRANILLO	Did you see anyone standing there? . . . Up the street . . . about seventy yards?
BRANDON	No.

immaculate perfect, without flaw.

GRANILLO	There was someone. There was a man. I saw him. I've remembered.	
BRANDON	Well, what of it?	40
GRANILLO	Oh, nothing . . . Brandon . . .	
BRANDON	Yes?	
GRANILLO	When I met Ronald. When I met him – coming out of the Coliseum – when I met him, and got him into the car – why shouldn't someone have seen us?	45
BRANDON	What do you mean by someone?	
GRANILLO	Oh, someone. Anyone. Did we think of that, Brandon?	
BRANDON	I did.	50

Granillo is now seated in armchair Left. Pause.

GRANILLO	Do you think we'll get away with it?	
BRANDON	When? To-night?	
GRANILLO	Yes.	
BRANDON	Are you suggesting that some psychic force, **emanating** from that chest there, is going to advise Sir Johnstone Kentley of the fact that the remains – or shall I say the lifeless entirety – of his twenty-year-old son and heir is contained therein?	55
GRANILLO	Listen!	60

There is a tense stillness.

BRANDON	What *are* –	
GRANILLO	Listen, I tell you! *(Another pause. Granillo springs up and goes over to window, where he can be seen peeping*	

---

emanating coming out of.

through the curtains.) It's all right. I thought it was **Sabot**. *(He comes down to chair again.)*

BRANDON	Sabot, in the first place, will not be here until five minutes to nine, if then, for Sabot is seldom punctual. Sabot, is the second place, has been deprived by a wily master of his key. He will therefore ring. Let me, I say, give you a **cool narration of our transactions**. This afternoon, at about two o'clock, young Ronald Kentley, our fellow-undergraduate, left his father's house with the object of visiting the Coliseum Music Hall. He did so. After the performance he was met in the street by your good self, and invited to this house. He was then given tea, and at six forty-five precisely, done to death by strangulation and rope. He was subsequently deposited in that chest. To-night, at nine o'clock, his father, Sir Johnstone Kentley, his aunt, Mrs Debenham, and three well-chosen friends of our own will come round here for **regalement**. They will talk small talk and depart. After the party, at eleven o'clock . . .
GRANILLO	*(interrupting)* This party isn't a **slip**, is it, Brandon?
BRANDON	My dear Granno, have we not already agreed that the entire beauty and **piquancy** of the evening will reside in the party itself? *(Pause.)* At eleven o'clock to-night, I was saying, you and I will leave by car for Oxford. We will carry our fellow-undergraduate. Our fellow-

---

Sabot Brandon's servant;
cool narration of our transactions a factual account of what we have done;
regalement entertainment; **slip** mistake; **piquancy** bitter-sweetness.

---

undergraduate will never be heard of again. Our
fellow-undergraduate will not be murdered. He   95
will be missing. That is the complete story, and
the perfection of criminality – the complete
story of the perfect crime.

---

1   With a partner, stage the opening scene from Rope.

2   Create a scene that uses the same devices as *Rope* to create
    dramatic tension. If you do not have access to stage lights or
    blackout facilities, focus on:

    • starting with a dramatic but unexplained event
    • use of whispers and sound effects
    • a character or characters in a state of extreme anxiety.

3   Analyse another play that you are studying to see if the
    playwright uses the device of dramatic irony. In *Romeo and
    Juliet*, for example, much of the tension and tragedy derives from
    the fact that the audience knows about Friar Lawrence's plan
    and knows that Juliet is not really dead, while Romeo is unaware
    of this.

Rope takes place in real time. This means that the action of the play is
a continuous narrative. The events that occur in the play take as long
as the play takes to perform. There are no gaps in the action. This is
an age-old tradition: the idea of the three unities (Time, Place and
Action) derives from Ancient Greek tragedy where one event triggers
the next, which triggers the next and so on. This is known as **linear
structure**.

The next extract, *Landscape of the Body*, was written in 1977
by American playwright John Guare. In contrast to *Rope*, the
action here moves backwards and forwards in time, using
flashback.

Landscape of the Body

ROSALIE Being dead is not the worst thing in the world. Is there life after death? I dare ask the question: Is there life before death. The good thing about being dead is at least you know where you stand. You have one piece of information in life and you think life means this. Then you get a new piece of info and everything you knew means something else. The scary thing about death is how comfortable it is. Finally giving in to the drowning. Life was always wriggling out of my hands like a fish you thought you had all hooked and ready to pop in the pan. Was there ever a day I didn't at one point say, 'Hey, when will life end?' Flashback! A new scene starring the boy who would soon be murdered.

Bert, a fourteen year old kid, swaggers on. He has ear phones on. He dances on to silent music.

This scene you are about to see contains information completely unknown to the boy's mother, my sister. Information unknown to Captain Marvin Holahan of the Sixth Precinct Homicide. Those two people in the course of their lives never learned the information you are about to receive right now. This scene takes place in the Parthenon. Not the one in Greece that's the cradle of all civilization. Hell, baby, I'm talking the Parthenon Luncheonette on West Eleventh Street and Bleecker in Greenwich Village. This scene takes place four weeks before this boy, my nephew, will be murdered.

A booth and table and chairs come in. Bert sits in the booth. His arm around one of the girls. Another boy, Donny, has his

sleeves rolled up wearing a lot of wristwatches. The girls
lean forward. The kids are roughly twelve, thirteen, fourteen.

BERT	It's so easy.
DONNY	Easy he says.
BERT	You stand on Christopher Street.
DONNY	I got to wait in the **tub**.
BERT	Pretty soon the guy stops.
DONNY	The tub gets cold. You got a cold ass waiting in the tub.
BERT	You noticed him cause he's walked back and forth a few times looking at you.
DONNY	All the things a tub can be. A coffin. I pretend I'm in a coffin.
JOANNE	Does he look at you like you're a girl?
DONNY	I pretend I'm in a boat.
JOANNE	Do they really look **fruity**?
BERT	Sometimes they are in cars. Not fruity cars, but Pontiacs. Oldsmobiles.
JOANNE	Fruits driving Pontiacs?
DONNY	I pretend I'm in a car.
MARGIE	I could see a Chevrolet. Chevrolets are fruity.
BERT	Not the '65 Chevy, Joanne. Holy shit, Joanne, I look at you sometimes and I say –
JOANNE	It was Margie who said it.
BERT	You were looking at her, agreeing with her.
JOANNE	Don't get mad at me. I'm sorry, Bert?
BERT	I don't like the two of you hanging around together. She's dragging you down. We all got to protect each other. Make each other better. Margie's dragging you down.

30
35
40
45
50
55

---

tub bath (American);   **fruity** derogatory term for homosexual.

Once again, the audience knows more than the characters. In this play too, tension and interest are sustained. The audience knows that Bert will be murdered but doesn't know when or why or who the killer will be. (By the way, you have probably noticed that Rosalie functions as a chorus, commenting on the action.)

4 Create a scene using flashback and a narrator commenting on the action, so that the audience knows more than the characters.

Another way of creating dramatic tension is to build a sense of anticipation within a scene. Try the following activity before you read the next extract.

5 Ask one person in the group to sit on a chair in a relaxed, comfortable manner. At a given signal, the person should transform their posture and movement (or lack of it) to indicate that they are waiting for someone to arrive or for something to happen, and that they are not looking forward to it. Take it in turns to be the person on the chair, and find different ways to build up the atmosphere. What happens if the person keeps looking at their watch? What happens if they get up and pace from time to time? If they glance at the door? Do these things create a more or less tense atmosphere?

The Country Wife is a Restoration comedy written by William Wycherley in 1676. Here, Mrs Pinchwife's brutal husband has made her write a letter to her lover. He exits to find sealing wax and candle, to seal the letter he has just dictated. This means that Mrs Pinchwife has only a limited time in which to act, and the audience's sense of anticipation builds dramatic tension.

 The Country Wife

PINCHWIFE   Come, wrap it up now, whilst I go fetch
             wax and a candle, and write on the
             backside, 'For Mr Horner.'

Exit Pinchwife.

MRS PINCHWIFE   'For Mr Horner.' – So, I am glad he has told
me his name. Dear Mr Horner! But why   5
should I send thee such a letter that will vex
thee and make thee angry with me? – Well, I
will not send it – Ay, but then my husband
will kill me – for I see plainly he won't let
me love Mr Horner – but what care I for my   10
husband? – I won't, so I won't send poor Mr
Horner such a letter – But then my husband
– But oh – What if I writ at bottom, 'My
husband made me write it'? – Ay, but then
my husband would see't – **Can one have no**   15
shift? Ah, a London woman would have had
a hundred presently. Stay – what if I should
write a letter, and wrap it up like this, and
write upon't too? Ay, but then my husband
would see't – I don't know what to do – But   20
yet **y'vads** I'll try, so I will – for I will not
send this letter to poor Mr Horner, come
what will **on't**.

She writes, and repeats what she hath writ.

'Dear, sweet Mr Horner' – so – 'my
husband would have me send you a base,   25
rude, unmannerly letter – but I won't' – so
– 'and would have me forbid you loving me
– but I won't' – so – 'and would have me
say to you, I hate you, poor Mr Horner –
but I won't tell a lie for him' – there – 'for   30
I'm sure if you and I were in the country at

Can one have no shift? Is there no plan available?;
y'vads an oath used by people from the countryside; **on't** of it.

cards together' – so – 'I could not help
treading on your toe under the table' – so
– 'or rubbing knees with you and staring in
your face till you saw me' – very well – 'and 35
then looking down and blushing for an
hour together' – so – 'but I must make
haste before my husband come; and now
he has taught me to write letters, you shall
have longer ones from me, who am, 40
dear, dear, poor, dear Mr Horner,
your most humble friend, and servant
to command till death,
Margery Pinchwife.'
Stay, I must give him a hint at bottom – so 45
– now wrap it up just like t'other – so –
now write, 'For Mr Horner' – But, oh now,
what shall I do with it? For here comes my
husband.

Enter Pinchwife.

6 Work with a partner to stage the scene, one acting and one
directing. How will you build dramatic tension? Use what you have
learned from previous activities in this chapter.

The final extract in this chapter demonstrates an unexpected **reversal**,
where the **dénouement** (or outcome) of the action takes a surprising
twist.

Softcops was written by Caryl Churchill and first performed in 1984.
The play is a montage of scenes on different aspects of crime and
punishment. The extract can be read as a complete – if very short –
play because this is the only time the audience encounters the two
conspirators.

Softcops

The stage is empty. Two Conspirators enter.

CONSPIRATOR A There's one way that can't fail.

CONSPIRATOR B What's that?

CONSPIRATOR A Throw myself under the horses' hooves with the bomb. Either it explodes straight off, or anyway the horses shy and there's a   5
delay and at that moment you go into action with the second bomb, so either way the whole thing goes up.

CONSPIRATOR B Either way you go up.

CONSPIRATOR A It can't fail.   10

CONSPIRATOR B You'd go that far?

CONSPIRATOR A Wouldn't you?

CONSPIRATOR B We can't afford to lose you. Too many of us are dead already.

CONSPIRATOR A Someone's betraying us, that's why.   15

CONSPIRATOR B Yes, someone's playing a double game.

CONSPIRATOR A It's hard to think one of your friends is a spy.

CONSPIRATOR B It's impossible. Everyone would give his life.

CONSPIRATOR A So everyone's equally under suspicion.

CONSPIRATOR B Even me. Even you.   20

CONSPIRATOR A Do you ever feel you can't go on?

CONSPIRATOR B You stop sleeping.

CONSPIRATOR A My stomach's water, my eyes itch. I'll be glad when it's over.

CONSPIRATOR B When you throw the bomb?   25

CONSPIRATOR A That or . . .

CONSPIRATOR B What? What?

CONSPIRATOR A	I sometimes think there's more spies than conspirators. Who plans the assassinations, us or them? Do we only murder so they 30 can arrest us?
CONSPIRATOR B	Listen, listen, what you've always said. However far control goes, subversion –
CONSPIRATOR A	We think we're subversive. They allow us.
CONSPIRATOR B	They kill one of us, two more – 35
CONSPIRATOR A	Do you believe it?
CONSPIRATOR B	It's what you've always said.
CONSPIRATOR A	I don't know.
CONSPIRATOR B	You're overtired. Let's get some coffee.
CONSPIRATOR A	It's me. 40
CONSPIRATOR B	What is? What?
CONSPIRATOR A	I can't go on. I'm the spy.
CONSPIRATOR B	Not you.
CONSPIRATOR A	Everyone's under suspicion.
CONSPIRATOR B	But not you. Not really you. 45
CONSPIRATOR A	Yes.
CONSPIRATOR B	Always?
CONSPIRATOR A	Yes.
CONSPIRATOR B	When you recruited me?
CONSPIRATOR A	Yes. 50
CONSPIRATOR B	When you assassinated the duke?
CONSPIRATOR A	Yes.
CONSPIRATOR B	But you're the one we all depend on.
CONSPIRATOR A	Yes.
CONSPIRATOR B	I was just an ordinary villain. You explained. 55 You said I could be a hero. And now what? What? All along? A spy all along? Michel's

death? And Marc, not Marc? And Louis
arrested last week, all you? But I'll tell
the others. We'll kill you. Why did you
tell me?   60

CONSPIRATOR A I was tired.

CONSPIRATOR B We'll kill you.

CONSPIRATOR A You won't tell the others. I feel better now.
Everyone has moments of weakness.   65

CONSPIRATOR B Of course I'll tell. I can't protect you.

CONSPIRATOR A I'm sorry I told you but it means I have to
kill you.

CONSPIRATOR B It doesn't.

CONSPIRATOR A Yes.   70

CONSPIRATOR B I won't tell.

CONSPIRATOR A Sorry.

CONSPIRATOR B Wait.

CONSPIRATOR A Yes?

CONSPIRATOR B Wait.   75

CONSPIRATOR A Hurry.

CONSPIRATOR B You'll laugh.

CONSPIRATOR A What?

CONSPIRATOR B You'll laugh. It's all right, old friend, it's all
right. The police are as full of secrets as we   80
are. To think I never knew. And you never
knew.

CONSPIRATOR A What?

CONSPIRATOR B It's me too. I'm a police spy too. So you
needn't kill me, all right? We just have to   85
go on keeping each other's secret and
doing our job. My dear old friend. I
thought Michel and Marc and Louis were

all my own work, and all the time it was you too. It is tiring, isn't it, the double life, twice as exhausting. What a relief to know. We'll never say another word about it, but we have each other now. We were always comrades, I always loved you, and how much more comrades now. How I love you now. Truth at last.

CONSPIRATOR A But I was lying, you see.

CONSPIRATOR B What?

CONSPIRATOR A I'm not a spy.

CONSPIRATOR B What?

CONSPIRATOR A You are.

CONSPIRATOR B What?

CONSPIRATOR A Sorry.

CONSPIRATOR B What?

Other Conspirators appear and B is killed.

---

7 In a pair, stage the scene using all you know about status and sub-text to make the unexpected dénouement as dramatically effective as possible.

8 Compile a list of the ways in which dramatic tension can be built, for use in your future work.

A11: Emoting

Different styles of play and different performance spaces require different performance styles. In this chapter, you will find out what style works best when, and why. Sometimes ***emoting*** – huge displays of anger, sorrow, fear and so on – is appropriate. On other occasions, a more restrained, low-key approach is called for.

The first extract is from a nineteenth-century melodrama, *The Colleen Bawn*, written by Dion Boucicault and first performed in 1860. 'Colleen bawn' is an Irish phrase for a pretty young woman. The second is from *Execution of Justice* by Emily Mann. This is a documentary drama, first performed in 1984 and concerned with the assassination in 1978 of Harvey Milk and John Moscone, two politicians in San Francisco. Most of the words in the play, including the speech reproduced here, are taken from evidence in the trial of the assassin, or interviews with people who knew the assassin and the assassinated. Both scenes involve characters in extreme emotional states.

The Colleen Bawn

CORRIGAN	Your humble servant, Mrs Cregan – it's a fine night entirely.
MRS CREGAN	May I ask to what business, sir, we have the honour of your call?
CORRIGAN	*(aside)* Proud as Lady Beelzebub, and as grand 5 as a queen. *(aloud)* True for you, ma'am; I would not have come but for a **divil of a pinch** I'm in entirely. I've got to pay £8,000 tomorrow, or lose the Knockmakilty farms.
MRS CREGAN	Well, sir? 10
CORRIGAN	And I wouldn't throuble ye –
MRS CREGAN	Trouble me, sir?
CORRIGAN	Iss, ma'am – ye'd be forgettin' now that mortgage I have on this property. It ran out last May, and by rights – 15
MRS CREGAN	It will be paid next month.

---

divil of a pinch difficult situation.

CORRIGAN	Are you reckonin' on the marriage of **Mister Hardress** and Miss Anne Chute?
MRS CREGAN	Mr Corrigan, state, in as few words as possible, what you demand. 20
CORRIGAN	Mrs Cregan, ma'am, you depend on Miss Anne Chute's fortune to pay me the money, but your son does not love the lady, or, if he does, he has a mighty quare way of showing it. He has another girl on hand, and **betune** the two 25 he'll **come to the ground**, and so **bedad** will I.
MRS CREGAN	That is false – it is a **calumny**, sir!
CORRIGAN	I wish it was, ma'am. D'ye see that light over the lake? – your son's eyes are fixed on it. What would Anne Chute say if she knew that 30 her husband, that is to be, had a mistress **beyant** – that he slips out every night after you're all in bed, and like **Leandher, barrin' the wettin'**, he sails across to his sweetheart?
MRS CREGAN	Is this the secret of his aversion to the 35 marriage? Fool! fool! what madness, and at such a moment.
CORRIGAN	That's what I say, and no lie in it.
MRS CREGAN	He shall give up this girl – he must!
CORRIGAN	I would like to have some security for that. I 40 want by tomorrow Anne Chute's written promise to marry him or my £8,000.

Mister Hardress Mrs Cregan's son, Master Hardress;
betune between; **come to the ground** come a cropper;
bedad an oath (by God); **calumny** false accusation;
beyant already;
like Leandher . . . wettin' in Greek mythology, Leander (sic) drowned while swimming across the Hellespont to see his lover.

MRS CREGAN	It is impossible sir; you hold ruin over our heads.
CORRIGAN	Madam, it's got to hang over your head or mine. 45
MRS CREGAN	Stay, you know that what you ask is out of our power – you know it – therefore this demand only covers the true object of your visit.
CORRIGAN	'**Pon** my honour! and you are as '**cute**, ma'am, as you are beautiful! 50
MRS CREGAN	Go on, sir.
CORRIGAN	Mrs Cregan, I'm goin' to do a foolish thing – now, **by gorra** I am! I'm richer than ye think, maybe and if you'll give me your *personal* 55 security, I'll take it.
MRS CREGAN	What do you mean?
CORRIGAN	I mean that I'll take **a lien** for life on *you*, instead of the mortgage I hold on the Cregan property. *(aside)* That's **nate,** I'm 60 thinkin'.
MRS CREGAN	Are you mad?
CORRIGAN	I am – mad in love with yourself, and that's what I've been these fifteen years.
MRS CREGAN	Insolent wretch! my son shall answer and 65 **chastise** you. *(Calls.)* Hardress!
CORRIGAN	You are in my power, ma'am. See, now not a **sowl** but myself knows of this secret love of Hardress Cregan, and I'll keep it as snug as a bug in a rug, if you'll only say the word. 70

'**Pon** upon; '**cute** acute, i.e. shrewd, intelligent; **by gorra** an oath (by Jesus);
a lien rights (i.e. he wants to marry her); **nate** neat;
chastise inflict punishment for the purposes of correction; **sowl** soul.

| MRS CREGAN | *(aside)* Scoundrel! he will tell her all and ruin us! *(loud)* Nothing. |

Turns aside.

 Execution of Justice

MILK'S FRIEND	After Harvey died, I went into a depression that lasted about a year, I guess. They called it depression, anyway. I thought about suicide, well, I more than thought about it. I lost my job. I stayed in the hospital for, I would guess, two months or so. They put me on some kind of drug that . . . well, it helped, I guess. I mean, I loved him and it was . . . Well, he was gone and that couldn't change. He'd never be here again, I knew that. 5
	10
	I had this recurring dream. We were at the opera, Harvey and I. I was laughing. Harvey was laughing. Then Harvey leant over and whispered: When you're watching *Tosca*, you know you're alive. That's when I'd wake up. And I'd realize – like for the first time all over again – he was dead. 15

---

1   Choose one of the scenes to rehearse and perform in the following two ways:

   a   First, ***intensify*** the action. To do this, *play the fact*. This means, decide what facts are presented in a scene. For example, in the speech by Milk's Friend the facts are:

   - that Milk is dead
   - that the speaker has been depressed and considered suicide
   - that the speaker dreams of Milk still being alive.

Your intention (see A5: Communicating, pages 19–22) should be *to inform* or *to communicate information*. You may think that this under-playing will reduce the emotional impact of the scene, but descriptions of awful events carry their own weight. Also, a person trying to keep calm, to keep their emotions under control, is often more affecting than a person in floods of tears.

b   In the second version, **magnify** the action. To do this, *play the emotion*. This means, decide what emotions a character begins the scene with and what emotions each speech or sentence creates as a response. For example, you might decide that in *The Colleen Bawn*, Corrigan begins by feeling vindictive (if you focus on his need for money) or lustful (if you focus on the fact that he has loved Mrs Cregan for fifteen years). You might decide that Mrs Cregan begins the scene fearful (because Corrigan has the power to evict her) or haughty (because she has higher status). The emotion will change in response to each line. For each emotion, choose a gesture or movement that will emphasise the emotion that is being expressed. You may want to underscore the scene with music, to heighten the atmosphere, as they did in the original nineteenth century melodramas.

In general, *magnifying* works best for plays whose style is large and bold and where emotions are expressed in words. *Intensifying* works best for pieces where there is a great deal of sub-text or whose style is more low-key. So, in theory, *Execution of Justice* should work best when intensified while *The Colleen Bawn* should work best when magnified. However, you may disagree. That's the great thing about Drama: there is plenty of room for interpretation.

Section B: Performance

B1: An Overview of the Rehearsal Process

As part of your GCSE Drama examination, you may be required to present a short play or an extract from a play. There are six such plays or extracts in Section B. All are a suitable length for this part of the examination (but check with your teacher as to the precise running time required); all feature between four and six performers. Each play in Section B has a short introduction about the author and the type of play that they have written, and a note on casting. It is followed by activities and ideas for discussion and written work, which will help you to explore that particular play.

Regardless of which play you choose (or even if you are not working on a play from this book), there are various general activities which will help to structure any rehearsal process. GCSE Drama students often think that the rehearsal process is about reading the play, learning the lines and performing it. But rehearsals are – or should be – about opening up different possibilities, trying out different ideas and different interpretations. So this overview is designed to give you ideas about that.

The following activities can be done in any order.

1   **Research what life was like at the time the play was written**. How is the world that the characters live in different from life nowadays? What inventions that we take for granted – cars, for instance, or electricity – would have been unknown to the characters? Which customs and ways of behaving are different from life nowadays?

2   **In your performance group, keep a rehearsal logbook**. Analyse the text. First, list facts about the characters and the play (it is a fact if there is evidence in the text to justify it). Include that evidence in your rehearsal logbook. Next, list your opinions and questions. All this will help you develop your ideas and interpretation of the play.

3   **Make sure you know what you are saying**. This seems like an obvious statement, but if the character uses words or phrases that

you are not familiar with, ensure that you understand exactly what they mean. If you are not clear what you are saying, how can you make it clear to an audience?

4 Use the following checklist to help you **understand the situation your character is in and how it affects that character**. This will give you options for how to perform a scene and the whole play. (Note: 'I' refers to the character, not the actor.)

- *Who am I?* All the facts you know about your character, or have imagined and decided.
- *Where am I?* Inside or outdoors? Alone or with other people? If outdoors, does the weather affect me? Is the place noisy or quiet? What sounds do I hear in the background? Is this a familiar place where I feel comfortable or a strange, hostile environment? What time of day is it?
- *What do I want?* Do I want something from the other person in the scene? Am I happy with my situation? Do I want to change it?
- *How do I get what I want?* Do I have to physically move to get it? Alter my body language? Change my tone of voice? Resort to drastic measures?
- *Why do I want it? What will happen if I don't get what I want?* Is it a small want or a big want? Will it make my day or my whole life better? Do I need whatever it is desperately, in order to carry on living?

The preceding questions are based on the work of Stanislavsky (1863–1938), who created a way of analysing character for actors which he hoped would lead to a simple, truthful style of acting.

5 **Create a time line for the play**. This will help you establish:

- what events, important or otherwise, occur between scenes
- what the audience knows that the characters don't
- what one or other character knows that another character doesn't
- how this creates dramatic tension.

6 **Tell the story of the play in five still images.** This should not be done too early in the rehearsal process. It will help you decide the *key moments* for the characters and for the audience, so that you know how best to mark and stage them. A key moment can also be described as a turning point, or a moment in the play on which the action pivots.

7 **Don't censor your imagination!** Collect images, pictures, anything that reminds you of the play, or the character, even if you're not sure why. Bring in pieces of music for the rest of the group to hear. Use your rehearsal logbook to share ideas. If the play or character was a drink, a fabric or an animal, what type of drink, fabric or animal would it be? Of what type of food or piece of music does the play or character remind you? You do not have to agree with each other; the important thing is to accept others' ideas and open up the possibilities.

8 All the activities in Section A can be applied to the character, relationship or text you are working on.

B2: Scenes from *The Rivals* by Richard Brinsley Sheridan (1775)

Richard Brinsley Sheridan was born in Dublin in 1751. In 1770 he moved to Bath, where *The Rivals* is set. In 1773, having fought two duels on her behalf, Sheridan eloped with Elizabeth Linley to France. He turned to playwriting as a means of supporting himself and his wife. *The Rivals* was his first play. The first version was a critical and commercial failure. Sheridan re-wrote the play in ten days – this second version was a huge success and has been part of the English-speaking repertory ever since.

The stylised and artificial form of an eighteenth-century comedy of manners was designed for that place and time. There was little attempt at realism or illusion. The characters openly acknowledge the audience's presence. The style of performance was loud, bold and presentational and took place downstage: it had to be like this, in order to hold the audience's attention. The auditorium remained brightly lit throughout the performance: the audience came to see and be seen as much as to concentrate on the play. That's why the uncut text of a seventeenth or eighteenth-century comedy has more re-caps than the average soap opera, designed as it was for those who had missed a particular scene or plot twist because they were gossiping, pursuing their love life, trying to fight a duel, or just jostling their way into the theatre.

Cast

Lydia Languish, an heiress.
Mrs Malaprop, her guardian.
Captain Jack Absolute, Lydia's lover.
Sir Anthony Absolute, his father.
The scenes that have been chosen form an extract suitable for four actors, two female and two male.

Lydia Languish, an heiress and avid fan of romantic fiction, is in Bath, with Mrs Malaprop, her guardian. Lydia wishes to marry for love not money. In consequence, wealthy Captain Jack Absolute disguises himself as Ensign Beverley, a poor soldier, to woo her. Unknown to Captain Absolute, his father, Sir Anthony, has approached Mrs Malaprop with a view to a match between Lydia and Jack. Jack (as himself) is obliged (as Ensign Beverley) to become his own rival. Hence the title.

ACT ONE Scene Two

> *Mrs Malaprop's* lodgings. Enter *Mrs Malaprop and Sir Anthony Absolute.*

MRS MALAPROP   There, Sir Anthony, there sits the deliberate simpleton, who wants to disgrace her family, and lavish herself on a fellow not worth a shilling!

Mrs Malaprop this character has given her name to 'the ludicrous misuse of words' (*Oxford English Dictionary*) – see below; the name comes from the word 'malapropos', meaning inappropriate.

LYDIA	Madam, I thought you once – 5
MRS MALAPROP	You thought, Miss! I don't know any business you have to think at all – thought does not become a young woman; the point we would request on you is, that you will promise to forget this fellow – to **illiterate** 10 him, I say, quite from your memory.
LYDIA	Ah! Madam! our memories are independent of our wills. It is not so easy to forget.
MRS MALAPROP	But I say it is, Miss; there is nothing on earth so easy as to *forget*, if a person chooses to 15 set about it. I'm sure I have as much forgot your poor dear uncle as if he had never existed – and I thought it my duty so to do; and let me tell you, Lydia, these violent memories don't become a young woman. 20
SIR ANTHONY	Why sure she won't pretend to remember what she's ordered not! Aye, this comes of her reading!
LYDIA	What crime, Madam, have I committed to be treated thus? 25
MRS MALAPROP	Now don't attempt to **extirpate yourself** from the matter; you know I have proof **controvertible** of it. But tell me, will you promise to do as you're bid? Will you take a husband of your friend's choosing? 30
LYDIA	Madam I must tell you plainly, that had I no preference for anyone else, the choice you have made would be my **aversion**.

---

illiterate *i.e. obliterate* wipe out completely;
extirpate yourself *i.e. exculpate* free yourself from blame;
controvertible *i.e. incontrovertible* cannot be overturned;
aversion strong dislike.

MRS MALAPROP What business have you, Miss, with
preference and *aversion?* They don't 35
become a young woman; and you ought to
know, that as both always wear off, 'tis
safest in matrimony to begin with a little
aversion. I am sure I hated your poor dear
uncle before marriage as if he'd been a 40
blackamoor – and yet, Miss, you are
sensible what a wife I made! – and when it
pleased Heaven to release me from him,
'tis unknown what tears I shed! But
suppose we were going to give you 45
another choice, will you promise us to give
up this Beverley?

LYDIA Could I **belie** my thoughts so far, as to give
that promise, my actions would certainly as
far belie my words. 50

MRS MALAPROP Take yourself to your room. You are fit
company for nothing but your own ill-
humours.

LYDIA Willingly, Ma'am – I cannot change for the
worse. 55

Exit Lydia.

MRS MALAPROP There's a little **intricate** hussy for you!

SIR ANTHONY It is not to be wondered at, Ma'am – all this
is the natural consequence of teaching girls
to read. Had I a thousand daughters, by
heaven! I'd as soon have them taught the 60
black art as their alphabet!

---

sensible aware of; **belie** misrepresent;
intricate *i.e. ingrate* ungrateful.

MRS MALAPROP	Nay, nay, Sir Anthony, you are an absolute **misanthropy**!
SIR ANTHONY	In my way hither, Mrs Malaprop, I observed your niece's maid coming forth from a 65 circulating library! She had a book in each hand – they were **half-bound volumes**, with **marble covers**! From that moment I guessed how full of duty I should see her mistress! 70
MRS MALAPROP	Those are vile places, indeed!
SIR ANTHONY	Madam, a circulating library in a town is as an ever-green tree of diabolical knowledge! It blossoms through the year! And depend on it, Mrs Malaprop, that they who are so 75 fond of handling the leaves, will long for the fruit at last.
MRS MALAPROP	Well, but Sir Anthony, your wife, Lady Absolute, was fond of books.
SIR ANTHONY	Aye – and injury sufficient they were to her, 80 Madam. But were I to choose another helpmate, the extent of her **erudition** should consist in her knowing her simple letters without their mischievous combinations; and the summit of her 85 science be – her ability to count as far as twenty. The first, Mrs Malaprop, would enable her to work A.A. upon my linen, and the latter would be quite sufficient to

---

misanthropy *i.e. misogynist* hater of women;
half-bound volumes books with a leather spine and corners;
marble covers the front and back cover of the book were covered with paper patterned like marble; **erudition** learning.

| | prevent her giving me a shirt, No. 1 and a   90 |
| | **stock**, No. 2. |

MRS MALAPROP   Fie, fie, Sir Anthony, you surely speak **laconically**!

SIR ANTHONY   Why, Mrs Malaprop, in moderation, now, what would you have a woman   95
know?

MRS MALAPROP   Observe me, Sir Anthony. I would by no means wish a daughter of mine to be a **progeny** of learning; I don't think so much learning becomes a young woman; for   100
instance – I would never let her meddle with Greek, or Hebrew, or Algebra, or **Simony**, or **Fluxions**, or **Paradoxes**, or such inflammatory branches of learning – neither would it be necessary for her to handle any   105
of your mathematical, astronomical, diabolical instruments. But, Sir Anthony, I would send her, at nine years old, to a boarding-school, in order to learn a little ingenuity and **artifice**. Then, Sir, she should   110
have a **supercilious** knowledge in accounts; and as she grew up, I would have her instructed in **geometry**, that she might know something of the **contagious** countries; but above all, Sir Anthony, she should be mistress   115
of **orthodoxy**, that she might not mis-spell, and mispronounce words so shamefully as

---

stock stiff type of neck-cloth; **laconically** *i.e. ironically*;
progeny *i.e. prodigy* a wonderful example;
Simony *i.e. cyclometry* a geometrical term for the measuring of circles;
Fluxions *i.e. fractions*; **Paradoxes** *i.e. parallaxes* an astronomical term;
artifice artfulness, trickery; **supercilious** *i.e. superficial*; **geometry** *i.e. geography.*
contagious *i.e. contiguous* adjoining; **orthodoxy** *i.e. orthography* correct spelling.

girls usually do; and likewise that she might **reprehend** the true meaning of what she is saying. This, Sir Anthony, is what I would have a woman know; and I don't think there is a **superstitious article** in it. 120

SIR ANTHONY
Well, well, Mrs Malaprop, I will dispute the point no further with you, though I must confess, that you are a truly moderate and polite arguer, for almost every third word you say is on my side of the question. But, Mrs Malaprop, to the more important point in debate – you say, you have no objection to my proposal. 125 130

MRS MALAPROP
None, I assure you. I am **under no positive engagement** with **Mr Acres**, and as Lydia is so obstinate against him, perhaps your son may have better success.

SIR ANTHONY
Well, Madam, I will write for the boy directly. He knows not a syllable of this yet, though I have for some time had the proposal in my head. He is at present with his regiment. 135

MRS MALAPROP
We have never seen your son, Sir Anthony; but I hope no objection on his side. 140

SIR ANTHONY
Objection! – let him object if he dare! No, no, Mrs Malaprop, Jack knows that the least **demur** puts me in a frenzy directly. My process was always very simple – in their younger days, 'twas 'Jack, do this' – if 145

---

reprehend *i.e. comprehend* understand;
superstitious *i.e. superfluous* extra, unnecessary; **article** item;
under no . . . **engagement** not committed to any agreement;
Mr Acres a friend of Captain Absolute's and a rival of Ensign Beverley;
demur hesitation.

	he demurred – I knocked him down – and if he grumbled at that – I always sent him out of the room.	
MRS MALAPROP	Aye, and the properest way, o' my conscience! – nothing is so **conciliating** to young people as severity. Well, Sir Anthony, I shall give Mr Acres his discharge, and prepare Lydia to receive your son's **invocations**; and I hope you will represent her to the Captain as an object not altogether **illegible**.	150 155
SIR ANTHONY	Madam, I will handle the subject prudently. Well, I must leave you – and let me beg you, Mrs Malaprop, to enforce this matter roundly to the girl, take my advice – keep a tight hand – if she rejects the proposal clap her under lock and key; and if you were just to let the servants forget to bring her dinner for three or four days, you can't conceive how she'd come about!	 160 165

Exit Sir Anthony.

ACT THREE Scene One

The North Parade. Enter Absolute.

ABSOLUTE	My father wants to force me to marry the very girl I am plotting to run away with! He must not know of my connection with her yet awhile. – He has too **summary** a method of proceeding in these matters	 170

---

conciliating *i.e. constricting*; invocations *i.e. imprecations* prayer, entreaty;
illegible *i.e ineligible* not fit to be chosen (as a husband); summary quick, brief.

and Lydia shall not yet lose her hope of an elopement. – However, I'll read my **recantation** instantly. My conversion is something sudden, indeed, but I can assure him it is very *sincere*. – *So, so* – here he comes. He looks **plaguy** gruff. 175

Steps aside. Enter Sir Anthony.

SIR ANTHONY No – I'll die sooner than forgive him. *Die*, did I say? I'll live these fifty years to plague him. – At our last meeting, his impudence 180 had almost put me out of temper. An obstinate, passionate, self-willed boy! Who can he take after? This is my return for getting him before all his brothers and sisters! – for putting him, at twelve years 185 old, into a marching regiment, and allowing him fifty pounds a year, besides his pay ever since! But I have done with him – he's anybody's son for me. – I never will see him more – never – never – never 190 – never.

ABSOLUTE Now for a **penitential** face. *(Advances.)*

SIR ANTHONY Fellow, get out of my way.

ABSOLUTE Sir, you see a penitent before you.

SIR ANTHONY I see an impudent scoundrel before me. 195

ABSOLUTE A sincere penitent. – I am come, Sir, to acknowledge my error, and to submit entirely to your will.

SIR ANTHONY What's that?

---

recantation renouncement; **plaguy** annoyingly or disagreeably;
penitential showing repentance.

ABSOLUTE	I have been revolving, and reflecting, and considering on your past goodness, and kindness, and **condescension to me**.
SIR ANTHONY	Well, Sir?
ABSOLUTE	I have likewise been weighing and balancing what you were pleased to mention concerning duty, and obedience, and authority.
SIR ANTHONY	Well, puppy?
ABSOLUTE	Why then, Sir, the result of my reflection is – a resolution to sacrifice every inclination of my own to your satisfaction.
SIR ANTHONY	Why now, you talk sense – absolute sense – I never heard anything more sensible in my life. – Confound you; you shall be *Jack* again.
ABSOLUTE	I am **happy in the appellation**.
SIR ANTHONY	Why, then, Jack, my dear Jack, I will now inform you who the lady really is. – Nothing but your passion and violence, you silly fellow, prevented my telling you at first. Prepare, Jack, for wonder and rapture – prepare. What think you of Miss Lydia Languish?
ABSOLUTE	Languish! What, the Languishes of Worcestershire?
SIR ANTHONY	Worcestershire! No. Did you never meet Mrs Malaprop and her niece, Miss Languish, who came into our country just

200

205

210

215

220

225

---

condescension to me talking down to me (Captain Absolute is being ironic);
happy in the appellation glad to be called so.

---

	before you were last ordered to your regiment? 230
ABSOLUTE	Malaprop! Languish! I don't remember ever to have heard the names before. Yet, stay – I think I do recollect something. – Languish! Languish! She squints, don't she? A little, red-haired girl? 235
SIR ANTHONY	Squints? A red-haired girl! Zounds, no.
ABSOLUTE	Then I must have forgot; it can't be the same person.
SIR ANTHONY	Jack! Jack! what think you of blooming, love-breathing seventeen? 240
ABSOLUTE	As to that, Sir, I am quite indifferent. If I can please you on the matter, 'tis all I desire.
SIR ANTHONY	Nay, but Jack, such eyes! such eyes! so innocently wild! so bashfully irresolute! 245 Not a glance but speaks and kindles some thought of love! Then, Jack, her cheeks! her cheeks, Jack! so deeply blushing at the **insinuations** of her tell-tale eyes! Then, Jack, her lips! O Jack, lips smiling at their 250 own discretion; and if not smiling, more sweetly pouting; more lovely in sullenness!
ABSOLUTE	*(aside)* That's she indeed. Well done, old gentleman! 255
SIR ANTHONY	Then, Jack, her neck. O Jack! Jack!
ABSOLUTE	And which is to be mine, Sir, the niece or the aunt?

---

insinuations hints.

SIR ANTHONY	Why, you unfeeling, insensible puppy, I despise you. When I was of your age, such a description would have made me fly like a rocket! The *aunt*, indeed! **Odds life**! when I ran away with your mother, I would not have touched anything old or ugly to gain an empire.	260 265
ABSOLUTE	Not to please your father, Sir?	
SIR ANTHONY	To please my father! Zounds! not to please – O my father! – **odso**! – yes – yes! if my father indeed had desired – that's quite another matter. Though he wa'n't the indulgent father that I am, Jack.	270
ABSOLUTE	I dare say not, Sir.	
SIR ANTHONY	But, Jack, you are not sorry to find your **mistress** is so beautiful.	
ABSOLUTE	Sir, I repeat it; if I please you in this affair, 'tis all I desire. Not that I think a woman the worse for being handsome; but, Sir, if you please to recollect, you before hinted something about a hump or two, one eye, and a few more graces of that kind – now, without being very **nice**, I own I should rather choose a wife of mine to have the usual number of limbs, and a limited quantity of back; and though *one* eye may be very agreeable, yet as the prejudice has always run in favour of *two*, I would not wish to **affect a singularity in that article**.	275 280 285

Odds life an oath (God's life); **odso** an oath (God's soul); **mistress** intended wife;
nice particular; **affect a singularity in that article** be different in that way.

| SIR ANTHONY | What a **phlegmatic sot** it is! Why, sirrah, you're an **anchorite**! – a vile insensible stock. You a soldier! – you're a walking block, fit only to dust the company's regimentals on – odds life! I've a great mind to marry the girl myself. | 290 |

| ABSOLUTE | I am entirely at your disposal, Sir; if you should think of addressing Miss Languish yourself, I suppose you would have me marry the aunt; or if you should change your mind, and take the old lady – 'tis the same to me – I'll marry the niece. | 295

300 |

| SIR ANTHONY | Upon my word, Jack, thou'rt either a very great hypocrite or – but come, I know your indifference on such a subject must be all a lie – I'm sure it must – come, now – damn your demure face! – come, confess, Jack – you have been lying – ha'n't you? You have been playing the hypocrite, hey! – I'll never forgive you, if you ha'n't been lying and playing the hypocrite. | 305

310 |

| ABSOLUTE | I'm sorry, Sir, that the respect and duty which I bear to you should be so mistaken. |

| SIR ANTHONY | Hang your respect and duty! But, come along with me, I'll write a note to Mrs Malaprop, and you shall visit the lady directly. | 315 |

| ABSOLUTE | Where does she lodge, Sir? |

| SIR ANTHONY | What a dull question! – only on the Grove here. |

---

phlegmatic cold, dull; **sot** blockhead; **anchorite** hermit.

| ABSOLUTE | Oh! then I can call on her in my way to the **coffee-house**. | 320 |

| SIR ANTHONY | In your way to the coffee-house! You'll set your heart down in your way to the coffee-house, hey? Ah! you leaden-nerved, wooden-hearted dolt! But come along, you shall see her directly – her eyes shall be the **Promethean torch** to you, – come along, I'll never forgive you, if you don't come back, stark mad with rapture and impatience – if you don't, egad, I'll marry the girl myself! | 325 |
| | | 330 |

Exeunt.

ACT THREE Scene Three

Mrs Malaprop's lodgings. Mrs Malaprop, and Captain Absolute.

| MRS MALAPROP | Your being Sir Anthony's son, Captain, would itself be a sufficient **accommodation**; but from the **ingenuity** of your appearance, I am convinced you deserve the character here given of you. | 335 |

| ABSOLUTE | Permit me to say, Madam, that as I never yet have had the pleasure of seeing Miss Languish, my principal inducement in this affair at present, is the honour of being allied to Mrs Malaprop; of whose intellectual | 340 |

---

coffee-house the eighteenth century equivalent of today's pub;
Promethean torch in Greek mythology, Prometheus stole fire from the gods and gave it to mankind; **accommodation** *i.e. recommendation*; **ingenuity** honesty.

accomplishments, elegant manners, and unaffected learning, no tongue is silent.

MRS MALAPROP Sir, you do me infinite honour! I beg, 345
Captain, you'll be seated. *(Sit.)* Ah! few
gentlemen, nowadays, know how to value
the **ineffectual** qualities in a woman! Few
think how a little knowledge becomes a
gentlewoman! Men have no sense now but 350
for the worthless flower of beauty!

ABSOLUTE It is but too true indeed, Ma'am – yet I fear
our ladies should share the blame – they
think our admiration of beauty so great, that
knowledge in them would be superfluous. 355
Thus, like garden-trees, they seldom show
fruit, till time has robbed them of the more
specious blossom. Few, like Mrs Malaprop
and the orange-tree, are rich in both at once!

MRS MALAPROP Sir – you overpower me with good- 360
breeding. He is the very **pineapple** of
politeness! You are not ignorant, Captain,
that this giddy girl has somehow contrived
to fix her affections on a beggarly, strolling,
eavesdropping **Ensign**, whom none of us 365
have seen, and nobody knows anything of.

ABSOLUTE Oh, I have heard the silly affair before. I'm
not at all prejudiced against her on that
account.

MRS MALAPROP You are very good, and very considerate, 370
Captain. I am sure I have done
everything in my power since I **exploded**

---

ineffectual *i.e. ineffable* inexpressible, unspeakable (because they are such good
qualities); **specious** lovely; **pineapple** *i.e. pinacle* top;
Ensign the lowest officer's rank in the army; **exploded** *i.e. exposed*.

| | the affair! Long ago I laid my positive **conjunctions** on her never to think on the fellow again – I have since laid Sir Anthony's **preposition** before her – but I'm sorry to say she seems resolved to decline every **particle** that I **enjoin** her. | 375 |

ABSOLUTE	It must be very distressing indeed, Ma'am.	380
MRS MALAPROP	Oh! it gives me the **hydrostatics** to such a degree! I thought she had **persisted from** corresponding with him, but behold this very day, I have **interceded** another letter from the fellow! I believe I have it in my pocket.	385
ABSOLUTE	*(aside)* O the devil! my last note.	
MRS MALAPROP	Aye, here it is.	
ABSOLUTE	*(aside)* Aye, my note indeed! O the little traitress Lucy.	390
MRS MALAPROP	There, perhaps you may know the writing.	

Gives him the letter.

ABSOLUTE	I think I have seen the hand before – yes, I certainly must have seen this hand before.	
MRS MALAPROP	Nay, but read it, Captain.	395
ABSOLUTE	*(reads)* '*My soul's idol, my adored Lydia!*' Very tender indeed!	

---

conjunctions *i.e. injunctions* orders, instructions, proposals;
preposition *i.e. proposition*;
particle *i.e. particular* profitable and/or advantageous match;
enjoin prescribe with great emphasis; hydrostatics *i.e. hysterics*;
persisted from *i.e. desisted from* stopped; interceded *i.e. intercepted*.

MRS MALAPROP	Tender! aye, and **profane** too, o' my conscience!
ABSOLUTE	'*I am excessively alarmed at the intelligence you send me, the more so as my new rival*' –
MRS MALAPROP	That's you, Sir.
ABSOLUTE	'*has universally the character of being an accomplished gentleman, and a man of honour.*' Well, that's handsome enough.
MRS MALAPROP	Oh, the fellow had some design in writing so –
ABSOLUTE	That he had, I'll answer for him, Ma'am.
MRS MALAPROP	But go on, Sir – you'll see presently.
ABSOLUTE	'*As for the old weather-beaten she-dragon who guards you*' – who can he mean by that?
MRS MALAPROP	*Me*, Sir – *me* – he means *me* there – what do you think now? But go on a little further.
ABSOLUTE	Impudent scoundrel! – '*it shall go hard but I will elude her vigilance, as I am told that the same ridiculous vanity, which makes her dress up her coarse features, and deck her dull chat with hard words which she don't understand*'–
MRS MALAPROP	There, Sir! an attack upon my language! What do you think of that? An **aspersion** upon my parts of speech! Was ever such a brute! Sure if I reprehend anything in

400

405

410

415

420

425

---

profane contemptuous, blasphemous; *intelligence* news;
vigilance watchfulness; **aspersion** damaging accusation.

	this world, it is the use of my **oracular** tongue, and a nice **derangement** of **epitaphs**!
ABSOLUTE	He deserves to be hanged and quartered! Let me see – '*same ridiculous vanity*' – 430
MRS MALAPROP	You need not read it again, Sir.
ABSOLUTE	I beg pardon, Ma'am – '*does also lay her open to the grossest deceptions from flattery and pretended admiration*' – an 435 impudent coxcomb! '*so that I have a scheme to see you shortly with the old harridan's consent, and even to make her a go-between in our interviews.*' – Was ever such assurance? 440
MRS MALAPROP	Did you ever hear anything like it? He'll elude my vigilance, will he? Yes, yes! ha! ha! He's very likely to enter these doors! – we'll try who can plot best.
ABSOLUTE	So we will Ma'am – so we will. Ha! ha! ha! A 445 conceited puppy, ha! ha! ha! Well, but Mrs Malaprop, as the girl seems so infatuated by this fellow, suppose you were to wink at her corresponding with him for a little time – let her even plot an elopement with 450 him – then do you connive at her escape – while I, just in the nick, will have the fellow laid by the heels, and fairly contrive to carry her off in his stead.
MRS MALAPROP	I am delighted with the scheme, never was 455 anything better **perpetrated**!

---

oracular *i.e. vernacular* native; **derangement** *i.e. arrangement*;
epitaphs *i.e. epigraphs* sayings; **perpetrated** put forward.

ABSOLUTE	But, pray, could not I see the lady for a few minutes now? I should like to try her temper a little.
MRS MALAPROP	Why, I don't know – I doubt she is not prepared for a visit of this kind. There is a **decorum in these matters**.	460
ABSOLUTE	O Lord! she won't mind *me* – only tell her Beverley –
MRS MALAPROP	Sir!	465
ABSOLUTE	*(aside)* Gently, good tongue.
MRS MALAPROP	What did you say of Beverley?
ABSOLUTE	Oh, I was going to propose that you should tell her, by way of jest, that it was Beverley who was below; she'd come down fast enough then – ha! ha! ha!	470
MRS MALAPROP	'Twould be a trick she well deserves – besides you know the fellow tells her he'll get my consent to see her – ha! ha! Let him if he can, I say again. *(calling)* Lydia, come down here! He'll make me a *go-between in their interviews*! – ha! ha! ha! Come down, I say, Lydia! I don't wonder at your laughing, ha! ha! ha! His impudence is truly ridiculous.	475 / 480
ABSOLUTE	'Tis very ridiculous, upon my soul, Ma'am, ha! ha! ha!
MRS MALAPROP	The little hussy won't hear. Well, I'll go and tell her at once who it is – she shall know that Captain Absolute is come to wait on her. And I'll make her behave as becomes a young woman.	485

---

decorum in these matters a proper way of doing things.

ABSOLUTE	As you please, Ma'am.
MRS MALAPROP	For the present, Captain, your servant – oh! you've not done laughing yet, I see – *elude my vigilance*! Yes, yes, ha! ha! ha! 490

Exit.

ABSOLUTE	Ha! ha! ha! one would think now that I might throw off all disguise at once, and seize my prize with security – but such is Lydia's caprice, that to undeceive her were probably to lose her. I'll see whether she knows me. 495

Walks aside, and seems engaged in looking at the pictures. Enter Lydia.

LYDIA	What a scene am I now to go through! Surely nothing can be more dreadful than to be obliged to listen to the loathsome addresses of a stranger to one's heart. I have heard of girls persecuted as I am, who have appealed in behalf of their favoured lover to the generosity of his rival: suppose I were to try it – there stands the hated rival – an officer too! – but oh, how unlike my Beverley! – I wonder he don't begin – truly he seems a very negligent wooer! Quite at his ease, upon my word! I'll speak first – Mr Absolute. 500 505 510
ABSOLUTE	Madam.

Turns round.

LYDIA	O heavens! Beverley!
ABSOLUTE	Hush! – hush, my life! – softly! be not surprised!

LYDIA	I am so astonished! and so terrified! and so overjoyed! For heaven's sake! how came you here?
ABSOLUTE	Briefly – I have deceived your aunt – I was informed that my new rival was to visit here this evening, and contriving to have him kept away, have passed myself on her for Captain Absolute.
LYDIA	O charming! And she really takes you for young Absolute?
ABSOLUTE	Oh, she's convinced of it.
LYDIA	Ha! ha! ha! I can't forbear laughing to think how her **sagacity** is overreached!
ABSOLUTE	But we trifle with our precious moments – such another opportunity may not occur – then let me now conjure my kind, my **condescending angel**, to fix the time when I may rescue her from undeserved persecution, and with a **licensed** warmth plead for my reward.
LYDIA	Will you then, Beverley, consent to forfeit that portion of my paltry wealth – that burden on the wings of love?
ABSOLUTE	Oh, come to me – rich only thus – in loveliness – bring no portion to me but thy love – 'twill be generous in you Lydia – for well you know, it is the only dower your poor Beverley can repay.
LYDIA	How persuasive are his words! How charming will poverty be with him!

Line numbers: 515, 520, 525, 530, 535, 540

---

sagacity widsom;
condescending angel angel in human form (i.e. descended from heaven);
licensed permitted.

ABSOLUTE	Ah! my soul, what a life will we then live?	545
	Love shall be our idol and support! We will	
	worship him with a monastic strictness;	
	abjuring all worldly toys, to centre every	
	thought and action there. Proud of	
	calamity, we will enjoy the wreck of wealth;	550
	while the surrounding gloom of adversity	
	shall make the flame of our pure love show	
	doubly bright. – By heavens! I would fling	
	all goods of fortune from me with a	
	prodigal hand to enjoy the scene where I	555
	might clasp my Lydia to my bosom, and	
	say, the world affords no smile to me – but	
	here – *(Embracing her. Aside.)* If she holds out	
	now the devil is in it!	

LYDIA Now could I fly with him to the Antipodes!   560
but my persecution is not yet come to a
crisis.

Enter Mrs Malaprop, listening.

MRS MALAPROP I'm impatient to know how the little hussy
deports herself.

ABSOLUTE So **pensive**, Lydia! – is then your warmth   565
abated?

MRS MALAPROP *Warmth abated!* – so! she has been in a
passion, I suppose.

LYDIA No – nor ever can while I have life.

MRS MALAPROP An ill-tempered little devil! She'll be in a   570
passion all her life, will she?

LYDIA Think not the idle threats of my ridiculous
aunt can ever have any weight with me.

---

abjuring foreswearing; **deports herself** *i.e. desports herself* behaves;
pensive thoughtful.

MRS MALAPROP	Very dutiful, upon my word!
LYDIA	Let her choice be Captain Absolute, but Beverley is mine.
MRS MALAPROP	I am astonished at her assurance! – to his face! – this to his face!
ABSOLUTE	*(kneeling)* Thus then let me enforce my suit.
MRS MALAPROP	Aye – poor young man! – down on his knees entreating for pity! – I can contain no longer. – *(Reveals herself.)* Why thou vixen! – I have overheard you.
ABSOLUTE	*(aside)* Oh, confound her vigilance!
MRS MALAPROP	Captain Absolute – I know not how to apologise for her shocking rudeness.
ABSOLUTE	*(aside)* So – all's safe, I find. – I have hopes, Madam, that time will bring the young lady –
MRS MALAPROP	Oh there's nothing to be hoped for from her! She's as headstrong as an **allegory** on the banks of Nile.
LYDIA	Nay, Madam, what do you charge me with now?
MRS MALAPROP	Why, thou unblushing rebel – didn't you tell this gentleman to his face that you loved another better? Didn't you say you never would be his?
LYDIA	No, Madam – I did not.
MRS MALAPROP	Good heavens! what assurance! Lydia, Lydia, you ought to know that lying don't

575

580

585

590

595

600

---

allegory *i.e. alligator.*

	become a young woman! Didn't you
	boast that Beverley – that stroller 605
	Beverley, possessed your heart? Tell me
	that, I say.
LYDIA	'Tis true, Ma'am, and none but Beverley.
MRS MALAPROP	Hold; hold, Assurance! you shall not be so
	rude. 610
ABSOLUTE	Nay, pray Mrs Malaprop, don't stop the
	young lady's speech: she's very welcome
	to talk thus – it does not hurt *me* in the
	least, I assure you.
MRS MALAPROP	You are too good, Captain – *too* amiably 615
	patient – but come with me, Miss – let us
	see you again soon, Captain – remember
	what we have fixed.
ABSOLUTE	I shall, Ma'am.
MRS MALAPROP	Come, take a graceful leave of the 620
	gentleman.
LYDIA	May every blessing wait on my Beverley,
	my loved Bev –
MRS MALAPROP	Hussy! I'll choke the word in your throat!
	Come along – come along. 625

*Exeunt **severally**, (Absolute) kissing his hand
to Lydia, Mrs Malaprop stopping her from
speaking.*

---

severally separately.

Activities and ideas for rehearsing *The Rivals*

The following can be done in any order.

1 Discuss how young women are expected to behave in the early twenty first century. Do the same expectations apply to young men? How do these present day expectations compare with how young men and women were expected to behave in the 1770s, as far as you can tell from the play?

Think about the techniques used in advertising or public information broadcasting. Use some of these to devise a piece called 'Do's and Don'ts for Young Women (or Young Men) in the Twenty First Century'. Use the same technique together with information from *The Rivals* and your research into the period in which it was written to produce a devised piece called 'Do's and Don'ts for Young Women (or Young Men) in the 1770s'.
Compare them. In particular, how similar or different are the relationships between the young characters in *The Rivals* and their parents (or guardians) and young people and their parents or guardians nowadays?

2 Whenever a play is heightened or artificial in form, there is a danger of playing the *style* rather than the *content*. If you emphasise fluttering fans, throwing back heads and laughing, delivering epigrams and funny lines as if you are a stand up comedian, you will lose the audience's interest. Of course, playing the scenes in a low-key, naturalistic way won't work either, but to succeed, the action must be founded on authentic characters and relationships. Make sure you look at B1: An Overview of the Rehearsal Process (pages 92–4) to ensure that you are clear on what the characters want and what's at stake. Use the activities in A11: Emoting (pages 84–9) as well.

3 The action of the play takes place in a single day. Read the whole play to see what else happens to your characters, in particular in between the scenes selected. How are you going to link these scenes? Think of a convention appropriate to the style of your performance and the play.

4 Find out about the design of such theatres as the Covent Garden Theatre, where *The Rivals* was first performed, and the Drury Lane Theatre (where Sheridan became the manager in 1776, having bought his share in the theatre with his profits from *The Rivals*). Draw a ground plan of the stage and auditorium and make notes to indicate why and how the design of the theatre contributed to the style of the performance.

5 Write diary entries for your character. Make sure you include the wrong words, if you are playing Mrs Malaprop!

6 The characters in *The Rivals* are stock types. Lydia is the romantic and impetuous heroine. Captain Absolute is the dashing devil-may-care hero. Mrs Malaprop is the snobbish and foolish elderly woman. Sir Anthony is the short-tempered and domineering old man. Watch a current TV comedy and/or analyse a comic play that you have studied.

- Which characters in current TV and film comedy use the same stock characters as *The Rivals*?
- To what extent does comedy depend on the use of stock types?

B3: An Edited Version of *Woyzeck* by Georg Büchner (1837)

Georg Büchner was born in Germany in 1813 and died in 1837. *Woyzeck* was first published in 1875, but it was not performed until 1913. The first translation into English was not made until 1927. The play is loosely based on an historical case: Johann Christian Woyzeck was beheaded in Leipzig in 1824 for murdering his mistress in a fit of jealous rage.

Although Büchner was only twenty-three when he died and only one of his three plays was ever performed in his lifetime, *Woyzeck* is perhaps the most original and influential work of theatre ever.

- In contrast to the kings and aristocrats that went before, Woyzeck is the first working-class tragic hero in world drama. The lives of characters such as Woyzeck, Marie and Andres are defined by poverty, although the author does not suggest this is a cause of or an excuse for murder.

- The language of the play is sometimes realistic, anticipating the fourth wall style of naturalistic drama about ordinary people's lives. Sometimes it is heightened and poetic, foreshadowing ***expressionism***. Expressionism is a form of theatre which creates an experience for audiences which communicates the mood and emotion of the leading character.
- The structure of the plot is episodic. Scenes – none lasting more than three minutes, some less than one – move from location to location and back again. The audience has to fill in the gaps. In this way, the play anticipates post-Second World War dramatists such as Caryl Churchill whose dialogue is terse and sub-text is hugely important.

Because the author died before the play was finished or revised, there is no definitive version. In fact, so illegible was Büchner's manuscript that it was not until 1927 that the name of the title character was correctly deciphered as Woyzeck not Wozzeck! The sequence of scenes varies from adaptation to adaptation. (In this book, the scene numberings have been edited for ease of use, and do not follow the sequence of the original.) Try to find at least two different versions to compare and contrast and to see what has been edited out in order to create a piece that five actors can perform.

Cast

Andres, soldier.
Woyzeck, soldier, with additional duties as **batman**.
Marie, Woyzeck's **common-law wife**.
Margaret, Marie's neighbour.
Drum-Major, specially privileged senior **NCO** used as a mascot and for recruitment purposes.
Showman

---

batman officer's servant;
common-law wife their 'marriage' is not recognised as legal by either Church or State;
NCO non-commissioned officer.

Sergeant

The Captain, for whom Woyzeck acts as batman.

Grandmother, very old. Blind.

Jew.

The following doublings are suggested:

1 (m) Woyzeck
2 (f) Marie
3 (m) Andres/Sergeant
4 (f) Margaret/Showman/Grandmother
5 (m) Drum-Major/The Captain/Jew.

Incidentally, Büchner may have been a revolutionary playwright but he was also shaped by the time he lived in. The pawnbroker who sells Woyzeck the knife, identified as 'Jew', reflects the anti-Semitic society of the times. To portray this society is not to endorse its values; however, you may prefer to change the name of the character to 'Pawnbroker'.

1

The woods. Andres is splitting sticks and whistling the tune of his song. Woyzeck enters.

WOYZECK   The place is cursed, you know, Andres. You see that light strip on the grass there, where the toadstools're so thick? A head rolls down it every evening. There was a man picked it up once, he thought it was a 5 hedgehog: three days and nights after, he was lying in his coffin.

(whispers) It was the **Freemasons**, Andres, I'm sure of it, the Freemasons.

Freemasons members of a mutual help society, who are sworn to secrecy as to the rituals etc. of the society.

| | – Quiet! | 10 |

ANDRES *(sings) A pair of hares were sitting there*
                Nibbling the green, green grass . . .

WOYZECK Quiet.
          Can you hear it, Andres? Can you hear it?
          Something moving. 15

ANDRES *Nibbling the green, green grass.*
          Until the ground was bare.

WOYZECK Moving behind me, beneath me –

He stamps on the ground.

Listen; it's hollow. It's all hollow under there.
– The Freemasons. 20

ANDRES It's scary.

WOYZECK So strange: still. 'Makes you hold your
          breath.
          – Andres!

ANDRES What? 25

WOYZECK Say something!

He stares out across the landscape.

Andres! How bright! It's all glowing above
the town, glowing. A fire raging in the sky
and clamour there below like trumpets. It's
coming this way! 30

Drags Andres into the bushes.

Quick! Don't look behind you!

ANDRES . . . Woyzeck? Can you still hear it?

WOYZECK Silence, nothing but silence; as if the world
          was dead.

ANDRES The drums're going, listen. We've got to get 35
          back.

2

*Marie and Margaret at Marie's window as the **retreat is being drummed**. Marie holds her child.*

MARIE   Hup, baby! Ta ra ra! – Hear it? – Here they come!

Precise and perfect, the Drum-Major marches the length of the street.

MARGARET   What a man, straight as a tree!

MARIE   And brave as a lion, I'll bet.   40

The Drum-Major gives an eyes right salute. Marie acknowledges.

MARGARET   Hey, that was a friendly eye you gave him neighbour! You don't treat every man to that.

MARIE   *(sings) Soldiers, they are handsome lads . . .*

MARGARET   Look at your eyes; still shining.   45

MARIE   So what? Take yours to the Jewman and let him polish them; you might be able to sell them for buttons if he c'n brighten them up.

MARGARET   Who're you to talk to me like that? Miss Motherhood! **I'm an honest woman, I am,**   50 **but you could see your way through seven pair of leather britches,** you.

She goes out.

MARIE   Bitch.
Well, baby, let them have it their way. After all, you're only the child of a whore,   55

---

retreat . . . drummed   the signal to retreat, given by drums;
I'm an honest . . . britches   implying that Marie will have sex with anyone.

---

unlucky thing; 'nd your wicked face just fills
your mother's heart with joy.

(She sings.) What shall you do, my pretty maid?
You've got a baby without a dad.
Never you mind about me –   60
All night long I'll sit and sing,
'Rockabye, rockabye, tiny thing,'
Though nobody cares for me.

WOYZECK comes to the window, knocks.

Who's there?
'That you, Franz? Come inside.   65

WOYZECK	'Can't. 'Got to go to **muster**.
MARIE	Have you been cutting wood f'r the Captain?
WOYZECK	Yes.
MARIE	What's the matter, Franz? You look so wild.
WOYZECK	There was something there again, Marie, a 70 lot of things.
	– Isn't it written, 'And behold, there came forth a smoke from the land like the smoke of an oven'?
MARIE	Oh, man! 75
WOYZECK	It followed me all the way to town. – What does it mean?
MARIE	Franz!
WOYZECK	'Got to go – See you at the fair this ev'ning.
	He leaves.
MARIE	That man! So haunted by everything. – He 80 didn't even stop to look at his child.

---

muster assembly, inspection.

Thinking's wound his mind up like a
watchspring, it'll break one'v these days.

– Why're you so quiet, baby? Are you
frightened?   85

It's so dark you could be going blind. – No
light.

The streetlamp usually shines in all the
time. These shadows, gathering like
deadmen . . .   90

It's horrible!

She hurries out with the child.

3

Marie and Woyzeck.
A Showman comes out of his tent.

SHOWMAN   – Roll up, ladies and gentlemen! Come and
see a monkey walking upright like a man!
He wears a coat and trousers and carries a
sword. Art improving on nature: our   95
monkey's a soldier. – Not that that's much.
Lowest form of animal life in fact.

No? Come and see the astronomical horse
then. Admired by all the crowned heads 'v
Europe. Tell you anything you like – how   100
old you are, how many children you've got,
what y'r illnesses are. Hurry now, the show's
just opening! Hurry now, roll up – it's the
commencemong of the commencemong!

---

commencemong mock French pronunciation of the English word 'commencement'.

| WOYZECK | Want to go in? | 105 |

| MARIE | I don't mind. – Yes, let's, there must be all kinds of things. |

They go into the tent as the Sergeant and Drum-Major enter the fairground.

| SERGEANT | Hold it. Look at that. – What a woman! |

| DRUM-MAJOR | Jesus, you could foal a cavalry regiment out of her. And breed drum-majors. | 110 |

| SERGEANT | Look 't the way she holds herself. That's what I call a body. All that meat to squeeze 'nd yet it moves as easy as a fish. Strange eyes – |

| DRUM-MAJOR | 'Make you think you're looking down a well, or a chimney. – Quick it's starting! Get in. | 115 |

They go inside and the Showman takes their money.

| MARIE | – So bright! |

| WOYZECK | In the dark – black cats with fires in their eyes. 'Strange night. |

| SHOWMAN | Observe: the unique phenomenon of the astronomical horse. | 120 |

– Show your paces now, show them y'r horse sense. Put humanity to shame.

Gentlemen, this animal you see before you with a tail and four hooves is a member of all the learned societies and, what's more, a professor at our university; where he teaches the students riding and kicking. | 125 |

That's a straightforward matter of understanding, though. | 130 |

– Now think inside-out. Show them what you can do when you use inside-out reasoning.

Is there an ass in this learned company?

The horse shakes its head responsively.

– See the effect of inside-out thinking? Done with **equine-imity**. Remarkable. This is no mute beast, I tell you; this is a person, a human being, an animalised human being – but still an animal. 135

The horse defecates.

That's it, put humanity to shame. – This animal's still in a state of nature, you see, of plain, unvarnished nature! You ought to take a lesson from him. Ask your doctor, it's positively harmful to be any other way! 140

The message is: Man, be natural. You were fashioned out of dust, out of sand, out of mud – would you be anything more than dust, sand, mud? 145

Look here, how about this for the power of reason? The astronomical horse c'n calculate, but he can't count on his fingers. Why's that? Because he can't express himself, can't explain – in fact, he's a human being **translated**! 150

– Tell the gentlemen what time it is.

Has any of you ladies or gentlemen a watch? – A watch? 155

SERGEANT A watch?

*Produces one from his pocket **magisterially**.*

---

equine-imity a pun on the word equanimity, meaning evenness of temper; 'equine' means relating to a horse; **translated** conveyed into another form; **magisterially** like a magistrate (i.e. done with authority).

	There you are, sir.
MARIE	I must see this!
DRUM-MAJOR	That's all woman. 160

The horse stamps its foot to tell the time.

SHOWMAN Eight o'clock! I ask you, is that not truly remarkable?!

– Ladies and gentlemen, this astonishing feat concludes the performance. Thanking you.

The Drum-Major and Sergeant watch Marie out as she passes them, followed by Woyzeck. The Showman attends to his effects.

SERGEANT Give the man a hand, soldier. 165

Woyzeck helps the showman. The Drum-Major follows Marie, who walks off by the woods. Eventually, the Sergeant lets Woyzeck go.

WOYZECK Marie?

Marie?

He runs out of the fairground. The Sergeant and Showman exchange looks.

4

Marie's room. She is tucking the baby into its crib.

MARIE The man gives him an order and he has to go, just like that.

She takes a piece of broken mirror from her blouse and examines the earrings she is wearing.

Look how they catch the light. I wonder 170 what they are? What'd he say?

– Go to sleep, baby, shut your eyes tight.

She bends over towards the crib.

Tighter. That's it. Now you keep still or else he'll come and get you.

(sings) Polly, close the shutter tight,   175
 A gipsy lad will come tonight.
 He will take you by the hand
 And lead you off to gipsy land.

– They must be gold!

An old crack in the back wall of a corner to   180
live in and a bit of broken glass to see with,
that's enough for the likes of us. My
mouth's as red as my lady's, though, for all
her full-length mirrors and rows of fine
gentlemen kissing her hand. An' I'm just   185
another poor girl.

– Sshh, baby, close your eyes. *(She **oscillates**
the fragment.)*

Here comes the sandman, walking across
the wall. Keep your eyes closed! If he looks
in them you'll go blind.   190

Woyzeck enters. Marie starts and covers her ears.

WOYZECK	What's that?
MARIE	Nothing.
WOYZECK	Under your fingers; it's shining.
MARIE	An earring. I found it.
WOYZECK	I never found that kind of nothing. Two at once, too.
MARIE	So? What does that make me?

195

---

oscillates gently waves.

WOYZECK   You're alright, Marie.

'Kid's well away, look at him. 'Ll just move
this arm so he doesn't get cramp.   200

Shiny drops, all over his forehead. –
Nothing but work under the sun; we even
sweat in our sleep. The poor.

– 'Some more money, Marie. My pay and
the extra from the Captain.   205

MARIE   God reward you, Franz.

WOYZECK   'Got to go. 'See you tonight. *(He goes out.)*

MARIE   Oh, I'm a bad bitch! I ought to cut my throat.
What sort of world d'you call this?

It's going to hell, all of it and us with it.   210

5

*The Captain on his chair awaiting a shave. Woyzeck
enters.*

CAPTAIN   Slowly, Woyzeck, take it slowly. One thing
after another one. You make me feel giddy.
– What am I supposed to do with the ten
minutes you save rushing that way? What
use are they to me?   215

Woyzeck starts shaving him.

Think about it, Woyzeck; you've got a good
thirty years left.

Thirty years. That makes three hundred and
sixty months – and then there's days,
hours, minutes! What're you going to do   220
with such a monstrous amount of time? Eh?

– Space it out a bit, Woyzeck.

WOYZECK	Yes, sir.
CAPTAIN	It makes me worried about the world, the thought of eternity. It's some business, Woyzeck, some business! Eternity . . . is eternity . . . is eternity – you can see that. But it's also not eternity, it's a single moment, Woyzeck, yes, a single moment. It's frightening, how the world turns round in a day. What a waste of time! What does it amount to? I can't stand to look at millwheels any more, they're so totally depressing.
WOYZECK	Yes, sir.
CAPTAIN	You always look so **wrought**! A good citizen doesn't look like that, Woyzeck, not a good citizen with a clear conscience.
	. . . Say something, Woyzeck. – How's the weather today?
WOYZECK	Bad, sir, bad. Windy.
CAPTAIN	I'll say. There's a real wind out there, I can feel it. 'Makes my back prickle, as if a mouse w's running up and down it.
	. . . *(slyly)* I should say it was a north-southerly.
WOYZECK	Yes, sir.
CAPTAIN	Ha ha ha! North-southerly. Ha ha ha!! – God, but the man's dense, horribly dense.
	You're a good fellow, Woyzeck, but *(solemnly)* you've no morals.
	Morals are . . . well, observing morality, you understand.
	That's the way of it. You've got a child

225

230

235

240

245

250

---

wrought worked up.

without the church's blessing, as our reverend padre calls it – without the church's blessing; that's his expression. 255

WOYZECK   Being poor . . .

said amen at the poor worm's making. The Lord said, '**Suffer** little children to come unto me'.

CAPTAIN   What do you mean? What an odd thing to 260 say.

What you said, I mean, not what he said.

– You're confusing the issue.

WOYZECK   Being poor . . .

D'you see, sir? Money, money! If you've no 265 money – Just you try getting one of our sort into the world in a moral way; though we're flesh and blood as well. We never get much luck, here or hereafter. If we went to heaven I expect they'd put us to work on 270 the thunder.

CAPTAIN   Woyzeck, you've no sense of virtue. You're not a virtuous man!

Flesh and blood?!

When I'm lying by my window, after it's 275 been raining, and I see a pair of white stockings twinkling down the street, hop-skip . . .

Dammit, Woyzeck, *I* feel desire then! I'm flesh and blood, too. But my virtue, 280 Woyzeck, my virtue! – So what do I do? I

---

without the church's blessing a double reference: Woyzeck and Marie are unmarried, and so their child cannot be baptised; **suffer** allow.

keep saying to myself: You are a virtuous man . . . *(maudlin)* a good man, a good man.

WOYZECK Yes, sir. I don't think virtue's so strong in me, sir. You see, people like us don't have any virtue, they only have what's natural to them. But if I was a gentleman and I had a hat and a watch and a big coat and all the proper words, I'd be virtuous alright. Must be a great thing, sir, virtue. Only I'm just a poor man. 290

CAPTAIN Well, Woyzeck, you're a good fellow, a good fellow. But you think too much. You're wearing y'rself out, grinding away 't things in there.

– You always look so wrought! 295

(Stands.) This discussion's upset me completely.

Get along now. *(Woyzeck removes the chair and his equipment.)*

And don't run! – Slowly. Nice and slowly down the street.

6

Marie's room. Marie and the Drum-Major.

DRUM-MAJOR Come on, Marie.

MARIE Show me again, go round the room. 300

He reproduces his parade-ground march.

The chest of an ox, with fur like a lion's mane. There's not another man like you. You make me proud to be a woman.

---

maudlin drunkenly tearful.

| DRUM-MAJOR | You should see me Sundays with my **plume** | 305 |

and **gauntlets**. That's really something.
'He's my idea of a soldier,' the prince
always says, 'A real man.'

| MARIE | Does he now? |

(Goes up to him, teasing.) A real man . . .? 310

*As he responds her mood changes and she moves
away.*

| DRUM-MAJOR | And you're a real woman. Christ, I'm going |

to fill your belly full of drum-majors, sire a
whole damn stable of them. Come on.

Grabs her. She struggles, violently.

MARIE	Let me go!
DRUM-MAJOR	Wild, eh? Come on then, animal.	315
MARIE	Just you dare.
DRUM-MAJOR	'Devil in you, isn't there? I can see it in your

eyes.

| MARIE | *(relaxes)* What's it matter anyway? It's all |

one. 320

7

*The street. The Captain. Woyzeck enters trying to
avoid notice.*

| CAPTAIN | – Hey! Woyzeck! |

Where're you dashing off to? Just wait there
a minute, Woyzeck. You go through the
world like an open razor. You'll be giving

---

plume i.e. on his helmet; **gauntlets** gloves which cover part of the arm.

someone a nasty cut one of these days. 325
Have you got to shave a regiment of
eunuchs on pain of death if you miss one
hair or something? Eh?

On the subject of hairs, that puts me in
mind of the saying – You know, Woyzeck – 330
The one about finding a hair from someone
else's beard in your soup. – You take my
meaning?

Or perhaps we should say in this case, from
someone else's moustache – a sapper's, or 335
a sergeant's, or, maybe, a drum-major's?

Eh, Woyzeck?

But then your wife's a good woman, isn't
she? Not like some.

WOYZECK Yes, sir. What do you mean, sir? 340

CAPTAIN Look at the man's face!

You might not find that hair in your soup,
but if you popped round the corner you
could just find it sticking to a certain pair of
lips. A certain pair of lips, Woyzeck. 345

Ah yes, I've known love in my time, too.

– Good God, you've turned to chalk, man;
you're stone white!

WOYZECK Captain, I'm a poor man – I've nothing but
her in the world. Please don't make jokes, sir. 350

CAPTAIN Make jokes? Me, make jokes with you?!

WOYZECK The earth's hotter th'n hell . . . and I'm cold.
Ice. Ice.

Hell must be cold, I'm sure. – It's not
possible! 355

Slut! Slut!! – Not possible.

CAPTAIN	What are you doing, staring at me like that? Do you want a bullet in the brain, man?! Your eyes're like knives.
	– I'm only doing you a favour, it's for your own good. Because you're not a bad fellow, Woyzeck, not such a bad fellow. 360
WOYZECK	I'm off. Anything can be possible. – The slut! Anything at all.
	– 'Fine day, Captain, isn't it? With a fine grey, stone sky. 365
	You c'd just hammer a peg in it and hang yourself.
	All because of the little pause between 'Yes' and 'Yes' again – and 'No.' 370
	Yes and No, Captain. – Is the No to blame for the Yes, or the Yes for the No?
	I sh'll have to think about that.

Moves away, step by step at first then increasingly quickly.

8

Marie's room. Woyzeck is staring at her with mad intensity.

WOYZECK	I can't see anything. Can't see anything.
	It should show! You should be able to see it, get hold of it with y'r hands! 375
MARIE	Franz? What's the matter? You're raving.
WOYZECK	What a fine street – you could wear your feet to stumps on it! It's good to stand in the street . . . Even better when there's company. 380

MARIE	Company?
WOYZECK	Lots'v people can walk down a street, can't they? And you can talk to them, to whoever you choose. And it's nothing to do with me!
	Did he stand here? – Then close to you? So? 385 Oh, I wish I'd been him.
MARIE	Him? – What're you talking about? I can't stop people coming down the street or make them wear muzzles, can I?
WOYZECK	And your lips're so beautiful – it's a shame 390 you couldn't leave them at home.
	But that would've brought the wasps in, I suppose.
MARIE	Well which wasp's bitten you then? You're like the cow th't the hornets stung. 395
WOYZECK	Such a sin. Such a great, gleaming, fat one – it reeks! You'd think the stink of it would bring the angels tumbling out of heaven.
	Your mouth's so red, Marie. Why're there no blisters on it? 400
	Why're you so beautiful, Marie? As beautiful as sin.
	Can mortal sin be beautiful?
MARIE	You're delirious.
WOYZECK	Did he stand here?! So?! Did he!?! 405
MARIE	Days're long and the world's old. A lot of people c'n stand in the same place, one after another.
WOYZECK	I can see him!!
MARIE	You c'n see lots'v things, if you've eyes 'nd 410 the sun shining 'nd you're not blind.

WOYZECK	*(goes to strike her)* – Slut!!
MARIE	Don't touch me, Franz!
	Put a knife in my guts if you want but not your hand on mine. 415
	My own father didn't dare do that when I was ten years old.
	He couldn't while I looked him in the face, and you won't now.
WOYZECK	Whore! 420
	No, it would have to show. – Everyone's an abyss. You get dizzy if you look down.
	Just suppose! – She walks like any innocent.
	Oh, innocence, there's a stain on your robe.
	Am I sure? Sure? – Who's ever sure? *(Goes out.)* 425

9

The guardroom. Andres is cleaning his boots and singing. Woyzeck is sitting down.

ANDRES	*The landlord has a pretty wife,* *Sits in the garden day and night;* *She sits in the garden waiting –*
WOYZECK	Andres!
ANDRES	What's now? 430
WOYZECK	A fine evening out.
ANDRES	Yeh, Sunday weather alright.
	There's some music later, over the heath. The women've gone up there already. 'Be some sweat shed, you can bet. 435
WOYZECK	Dancing, Andres. They'll be dancing!

ANDRES	At The Horse 'nd The Star, that's right.
WOYZECK	Dancing, dancing!
ANDRES	Why not?
	(sings) She sits in the garden waiting – 440
	Until the village clock strikes twelve
	And the soldier-boys come marching.
WOYZECK	Andres – I can't get any rest from it.
ANDRES	More fool you.
WOYZECK	Her hands'll be hot. – Oh damn her, 445
	Andres, damn her!

Marie and the Drum-Major appear outside, dancing.

Him. Her.

Hell. – Hell, hell!

They spin a long, elaborate revolve.

MARIE	On and on –
DRUM-MAJOR	Round and round – 450
MARIE	For ever and ever –
	On and on and on . . .
WOYZECK	'Got to go. 'See for myself.
ANDRES	Why make trouble? Over one like that.
WOYZECK	'Got to get out. It's stifling. *(Goes)* 455

10

The woods beyond.

WOYZECK	On and on! For ever! On, on, on!
	Stop the music. – Shh.
	(throws himself down) What's that? – What's

that you say? What're you saying?

. . . Stab . . . Stab the she-wolf, dead.   460

Shall I?

Must I?

– Is it there, too? In the wind even.

(Stands up.) It's all round me. Everywhere.
Round, round, on and on and on . . .   465

Stab her. Dead, dead – dead!! *(Runs out.)*

11

The guardroom. Andres asleep in a blanket. Woyzeck comes in, shakes him.

WOYZECK   Andres, Andres! – I can't sleep. Everything
starts spinning when I shut my eyes and I
hear the fiddles – on and on, round and
round. Then it says it again, out of the wall.   470
Can you hear it?

ANDRES   *(mumbles)* Yes, yes; let th'm dance.

(Turns over.) 'Man gets tired. God save us. Amen.

WOYZECK   Always the same – stab, stab!

Between my eyes. Like a knife.   475

ANDRES   Get to bed, y'fool.

Goes back to sleep. Woyzeck goes out.

12

The tavern, late. The Drum-Major is seated alone at one side. Others grouped carefully away from him. Woyzeck.

DRUM-MAJOR   I'm a man! *(Pounds his chest.)*

A man! D'you hear? – Who's looking f'r a
fight? If y're not 's pissed 's creeping Jesus
keep away from me. I'll ram y'r nose up   480
your arse!

(to Woyzeck) Hey, you, drink up. Everyone has
to drink. Drink. I wish the world w's made
'v schnapps, me, schnapps – I said,
everyone has to drink. You: drink.   485

Woyzeck whistles.

You little shit.

I'll rip the tongue from y'r throat and
strangle you with it.

*Throws himself on Woyzeck, who takes a bad beating
in the ensuing fight. It ends with him on the ground.*

Bastard; rat turd. I'm going to knock the
breath out'v you alright. You won't have   490
enough f'r an old woman's fart.

Jumps on Woyzeck's back with his knees.

– Now try and whistle, shit. You c'n whistle
y'rself sky-blue f'r all I care.

(sings) Oh – brandy is the drink for me;

Brandy gives a man spunk!   495

Goes for more drink. The crowd feel free to talk.

13

*Morning, the guardroom. Andres with a towel.
Woyzeck comes in to him.*

WOYZECK   Was he in the washroom? Did he say
          anything?

ANDRES	*(dries his face)* He w's with his mates.
WOYZECK	What'd he say? What'd he *say*?
ANDRES	What's the difference?

What d'you want him to say – a red-hot piece, fantastic, h'r inside's like running butter?

WOYZECK	*(cold)* So that's what he said.

What was I dreaming about last night? A knife, was it? Stupid things, dreams.

Gathers his kit up.

ANDRES	Where're you off to?
WOYZECK	'Fetch my officer's wine.

– But you know, Andres, there was no-one like her.

ANDRES	Who?
WOYZECK	'Doesn't matter. – 'See you.

He goes out.

14

The Jew in his shop. Woyzeck enters.

WOYZECK	Any guns?
JEW	Maybe.
WOYZECK	How much?
JEW	Four crowns, five crowns. How much you got?
WOYZECK	'S too dear.
JEW	You buy, you don't buy. Which?
WOYZECK	How much for a knife?

JEW	This one?
	Lovely straight, this one. – You want to cut your throat with it? So, what's that? I give you cheap – same price as anyone else. Cheap you can have your death; not for nothing. So, what's that? You get death economical.
WOYZECK	*(feels)* It'll cut more th'n bread.
JEW	Two **groschen**.
WOYZECK	Take it.

Pushes the money into his hand and goes.

JEW	Take it!
	Just like that: as if it was nothing. – And it's money, all of it money.
	Dog!

15

Marie's room. The child is in its crib, Marie knelt nearby with an open Bible.

MARIE	'. . . *Neither was guile found in his mouth.*'
	Don't look at me, Lord.

She turns to another page.

'And the scribes and the pharisees brought unto him a woman taken in adultery, and set her in the midst . . . And Jesus said unto her, Neither do I condemn thee. Go, and sin no more.'

525

530

535

540

groschen a small silver coin in use in some German-speaking areas in the 19th century.

Tries to hold her hands together in prayer.

I can't. – Can't.

Dear God, don't take everything, at least let me pray.

The child stirs and she comforts him.

And Franz doesn't come. Yesterday, today. 'Still doesn't come. 545

– It gets so hot!

Goes to the window and opens it, comes back to the Bible. She picks it up and reads where she's standing.

'. . . And she stood at his feet behind him weeping, and began to wash his feet with tears and did wipe them with the hairs of 550 her head, and kissed his feet and anointed them with an ointment.'

Strikes herself on the breast.

Dead; all dead! – Oh my Lord, my Lord!

If only I could anoint your feet.

16

The guardroom. Woyzeck is going through his kitbag, Andres watching.

WOYZECK This waistcoat's not standard issue, Andres. 555 You might be able to use it for something.

The cross belongs to my sister, so does the ring. I've got a holy picture somewhere too, a pair of twined hearts – my mother used to keep it in her Bible. There's a motto: Christ, 560 as your heart was red and wounded, so let mine be cleft and sundered. She's no feeling left, my mother, only when the sun shines on h'r hands.

– Doesn't matter.   565

ANDRES 'Course.

WOYZECK *(pulls out a sheet of paper)* 'Friedrich Johann Franz Woyzeck. Rifleman. Second Fusiliers Regiment, Second Battalion, Fourth Company. Born on the **Feast of The**   570
Annunciation – '

I'm thirty years old. Thirty years, seven months and twelve days.

ANDRES You ought to report sick, Franz, you're not right. Have a **schnapps** with powder in it to   575
kill the fever.

WOYZECK That's it, Andres.

When the carpenter collects his shavings for the box, no-one knows whose head'll lie on them.   580

17

The street. Marie standing by the Grandmother, seated.

GRANDMOTHER Sing, Marie.

MARIE No.

GRANDMOTHER Why not?

Feast of The Annunciation 25 March; **schnapps** a type of spirits.

MARIE	Because.	
GRANDMOTHER	Because what?	585
MARIE	Just because.	
GRANDMOTHER	All right, Grandma'll tell you a story. Sit, sit.	

GRANDMOTHER Once upon a time there was a poor little boy who had no father and mother; everything was dead and there was no-one 590 left in the whole world. Everything was quite dead, so he went off, whimpering. All day and all night. And since there was no-one left on earth he decided to go up to heaven where the moon shone down so 595 kind. But when he got to the moon it was a lump of rotten wood. Then he went to the sun, but when he got there it was a withered-up sunflower. And when he got to the stars they were little spangled midges 600 stuck there, like the ones **shrikes** stick on blackthorns. So he went back to the earth, but the earth was an overturned pot. He was completely alone, and he sat down and cried. He's sitting there still, all alone. 605

Woyzeck comes into the street.

WOYZECK	Marie!	
MARIE	*(starts)* What is it?	
WOYZECK	We've got to go, Marie, it's time.	
MARIE	Go where?	
WOYZECK	Does it matter?	610

They go down the street.

---

shrikes a type of bird.

18

The woods. Woyzeck and Marie come through them slowly.

MARIE	The town's that way. It's dark.
WOYZECK	Stay a bit. Here, sit down.
MARIE	I've got to get back.
WOYZECK	You won't get sore feet from walking. I'll save you that.

615

MARIE	What're you on about?
WOYZECK	D'you know how long it's been, Marie?
MARIE	Two years this **Whitsun**.
WOYZECK	D'you know how long it's going to be?
MARIE	I've got to go, there's supper to get.

620

WOYZECK	Are you cold, Marie?
	'Nd yet you're warm! – And you've hot lips, hot breath. Hot, hot whore's breath! I'd give heav'n to kiss them again, though.

	When we're really cold, then we don't feel the weather any more. You won' feel the damp in the morning.

625

MARIE	What's that you say?
WOYZECK	Nothing.

A silence.

MARIE	The moon's up. 'All red.

630

WOYZECK	Like blood on iron.
MARIE	What d'you mean? – Franz, you're so pale.

He draws the knife.

Whitsun the seventh weekend after Easter.

No, Franz!

Merciful God. Help! Help!

He stabs her.

WOYZECK There! There! There! 635

Why don't you die? – Die, die!!

– Ha, still moving? Even now; even now?

He holds the head back and cuts her throat.

Still moving?

Lets the body fall.

Now are you dead? Now?

Dead. Dead. Dead. 640

He kneels on one knee by the body. Pulls the trunk up onto him resting her back on his knee, holding her like a child.

WOYZECK Why're you so pale, Marie?

What's that red thing round your neck? Is it a necklace?

Who gave you a necklace to commit sins with him? 645

Oh, you were black with them, black.

Have I made you white again?

Why's your hair so wild, Marie? – Didn't you comb it today?

So, I'll tidy it for you. You have to look your 650
best, there'll be people to meet.

What're all these marks? Look. Here, here.
Like bloodstains. How did you get them?
Have you been fighting, Marie?

Starts to lift the body.

You have to get up now, then I can wash you. 655
It's not far. Up.

Stands upright with the body held in front of him.

There's water here, to wash you. To wash
everything away, then you'll be clean. –
Come to the water.

Drags her down to the pool side.

D'you see the moon, Marie? There's even 660
blood on the moon. But you'll be clean.

Take a step. Then another.

And another.

Another.

– Water, Marie. All the water in the world to 665
wash you. Water –

They disappear into the pool. Silence.

Activities and ideas for rehearsing *Woyzeck*

The following can be done in any order.

1 While the style of the play is fragmented, the action needs to be
   fluid. A challenge for the group staging the piece is how to balance
   these things. Consider using blackouts between scenes. Also think
   about how to indicate to the audience the different locations
   where the play takes place, without having to stop the action and
   move scenery and furniture.

2 Apply the activities on sub-text in A9: Revealing (pages 64–70) and
   on building tension in A10: Building (pages 70–84) to *Woyzeck* as
   part of your rehearsal process. This will help you create the
   atmosphere of brooding tension that the play requires.

3   Prepare an improvised version of the play as a television soap opera. Do you need additional or different characters to tell the story in this way?

4   Because the audience sees brief snapshots of the action, there are gaps between the scenes in the play. As actors, you need to be clear on what has happened between scenes. Improvise the scenes that we do not see.

5   *Woyzeck* uses folk songs, the pop music of its day. What is the function of these songs? If you were going to substitute contemporary pop music, what songs would you choose and why?

6   Although the relationship between Marie and Woyzeck is central, all the other characters in the play have relationships with one or both of them, however briefly. To help these actors understand and communicate these relationships, write a monologue for each character apart from Woyzeck and Marie. The character should be looking back on the events of the play after Woyzeck has murdered Marie and killed himself. Consider:

   • the character's attitude to the events and the two characters
   • whether the character feels guilty or responsible
   • how that feeling (or the lack of feeling) affects what the character says and how they say it.

B4: *The Actor's Nightmare* by Christopher Durang (1981)

Christopher Durang is an American playwright who was born in 1949. He writes savage comedies, which use laughter to attack such things as the myth of the happy family (*The Marriage of Bette and Boo*), organised religion (*Sister Mary Ignatius Explains It All For You*) or the counselling and psychiatry industry (*Beyond Therapy*). *The Actor's Nightmare* is a lighter piece, based on a nightmare that most actors have had, often when rehearsals are not going well. In this nightmare, the actor is on stage in front of an audience, not knowing what the lines are and – in the case of this play – not even being an actor, or knowing what the play is, or why it keeps changing into a different play!

The Actor's Nightmare also uses the convention of the **play-within-a-play**. You may recognise this from other plays as different as *A Midsummer Night's Dream* by William Shakespeare (c. 1595), *Forty Years On* by Alan Bennett (1968), *Noises Off* by Michael Frayn (1982) and *Our Country's Good* by Timberlake Wertenbaker (1988).

Cast

George Spelvin, an accountant.
Meg, a stage manager.
Sarah Siddons, a grand actress.
Ellen Terry, another actress (not as grand).
Henry Irving, a grand actor.
The Executioner.

The play can be performed by five actors (if the parts of Henry Irving and The Executioner are doubled) or six (if they are not). Any actor can play the Voice. You don't need to perform the play with American accents, because the actor's nightmare is a universal one.

The author suggests that the character of the Executioner should not be listed in the programme. If you have read about the concept of reversal in *Softcops* in A10: Building (pages 80–4) you will understand why, once you have read *The Actor's Nightmare*.

Incidentally, another joke is that the actors in the play are all named after great actors from history. Sarah Siddons (1755–1831) was the most acclaimed tragic actress of her day. Sir Henry Irving (1835–1905) was an actor-manager and the first actor to be knighted. Ellen Terry (1847–1928) was Irving's leading lady for much of her career.

Scene: Basically an empty stage, maybe with a few set pieces on it or around it. George Spelvin, a young man, wanders in. He looks baffled and uncertain where he is. Enter Meg, the stage manager. In jeans and sweatshirt, perhaps, pleasant, efficient.

GEORGE   Oh, I'm sorry. I don't know how I got in here.

MEG   Oh, thank goodness you're here. I've been calling you.

GEORGE   Pardon?   5

MEG   An awful thing has happened. Eddie's been in a car accident, and you'll have to go on for him.

GEORGE   Good heavens, how awful. Who's Eddie?

MEG   Eddie.   10

He looks blank.

MEG   Edwin. You have to go on for him.

GEORGE   On for him.

MEG   Well, he can't go on. He's been in a car accident.

GEORGE   Yes I understood that part. But what do you 15 mean 'go on for him'?

MEG   You play the part. Now I know you haven't had a chance to rehearse it exactly, but presumably you know your lines, and you've certainly seen it enough.   20

GEORGE   I don't understand. Do I know you?

MEG   George, we really don't have time for this kind of joshing. Half-hour. *(Exits.)*

GEORGE   My name isn't George, it's . . . well, I don't know what it is, but it isn't George. 25

Enter Sarah Siddons, a glamorous actress, perhaps in a sweeping cape.

SARAH	My God, did you hear about Eddie?
GEORGE	Yes I did.
SARAH	It's just too, too awful. Now good luck tonight, George darling, we're all counting on you. Of course, you're a little too young (30) for the part, and you are shorter than Edwin so we'll cut all the lines about bumping your head on the ceiling. And don't forget when I cough three times, that's your cue to unzip the back of my dress and then I'll slap you. (35) We changed it from last night. *(She starts to exit.)*
GEORGE	Wait, please. What play are we doing exactly?
SARAH	*(stares at him)* What?
GEORGE	What is the play, please?
SARAH	Coward. (40)
GEORGE	Pardon?
SARAH	Coward. *(Looks at him as if he's crazy.)* It's the Coward. Noël Coward. *(suddenly relaxing)* George, don't do that. For a second, I thought you were serious. Break a leg, (45) darling. *(Exits.)*
GEORGE	*(to himself)* Coward. I wonder if it's *Private Lives.* At least I've seen that one. I don't remember rehearsing it exactly. And am I an actor? I thought I was an accountant. And (50) why does everyone call me George?

Enter Dame Ellen Terry, younger than Sarah, a bit less grand.

ELLEN	Hello, Stanley. I heard about Edwin. Good luck tonight. We're counting on you.

GEORGE	Wait, what play are we doing?
ELLEN	Very funny, Stanley. 55
GEORGE	No really, I've forgotten.
ELLEN	*Checkmate.*
GEORGE	*Checkmate?*
ELLEN	By Samuel Beckett. You know, in the garbage cans. You always play these jokes, Stanley, 60 just don't do it onstage. Well, good luck tonight. I mean, break a leg. Did you hear? Edwin broke *both* legs. *(Exits.)*
GEORGE	I've never heard of *Checkmate*.

Re-enter Meg.

| MEG | George, get into costume. We have fifteen 65 minutes. *(Exits.)* |

Enter Henry Irving, age 28–33, also somewhat grand.

HENRY	Good God, I'm late. Hi, Eddie. Oh you're not Eddie. Who are you?
GEORGE	You've never seen me before?
HENRY	Who the devil are you? 70
GEORGE	I don't really know. George, I think. Maybe Stanley, but probably George. I think I'm an accountant.
HENRY	Look, no one's allowed backstage before a performance. So you'll have to leave, or I'll 75 be forced to report you to the stage manager.
GEORGE	Oh she knows I'm here already.
HENRY	Oh. Well, if Meg knows you're here it must be all right I suppose. It's not my affair. I'm 80 late enough already. *(Exits.)*

MEG	*(offstage)* Ten minutes, everybody. The call is ten minutes.
GEORGE	I better just go home. *(Takes off his **pants**.)* Oh dear, I didn't mean to do that.

Enter Meg.

MEG	George, stop that. Go into the dressing room to change. Really, you keep this up and we'll bring you up on charges.
GEORGE	But where is the dressing room?
MEG	George, you're not amusing. It's that way. And give me those. *(Takes his pants.)* I'll go soak them for you.
GEORGE	Please don't soak them.
MEG	Don't tell me my job. Now go get changed. The call is five minutes. *(Pushes him off to dressing room; crosses back the other way, calling out.)* Five minutes, everyone. Five minutes. Places.

A curtain closes on the stage. Darkness. Lights come up on the curtain. A voice is heard.

VOICE	Ladies and gentlemen, may I have your attention please? At this evening's performance, the role of Elyot, normally played by Edwin Booth, will be played by George Spelvin.

Sound of audience moans.

The role of Amanda, normally played by **Sarah Bernhardt**, will be played by

---

pants trousers (American);
Sarah Bernhardt a French actress (1845–1923).

Sarah Siddons. The role of Kitty the bar 105
maid will be played by **Mrs Patrick
Campbell**. **Dr Crippin** will play himself. The
management wishes to remind the audience
that the taking of photographs is strictly
forbidden by law, and is dangerous as it may 110
disorient the actor. Thank you.

*The curtain opens. There is very little set, but probably
a small set piece to indicate the railing of a terrace
balcony. Some other set piece (a chair, a table, a
cocktail bar) might be used to indicate wealth,
elegance, French Riviera.*

*Sarah Siddons is present when the curtain opens. She
is in a glamorous evening gown, and is holding a
cocktail glass and standing behind the terrace railing,
staring out above the audience's head. There is the
recorded sound of applause.*

*After a moment George arrives onstage, fairly pushed
on. He is dressed as Hamlet – black leotard and large
gold medallion around his neck. As soon as he enters,
several flash photos are taken, which disorient him
greatly. When he can, he looks out and sees the
audience and is very taken aback. We hear music.*

SARAH   Extraordinary how potent cheap music is.

GEORGE   What?

SARAH   Extraordinary how potent cheap music is.

GEORGE   Yes, that's true. Am I supposed to be Hamlet? 115

SARAH   *(alarmed; then going on)* Whose yacht do you
think that is?

Mrs Patrick Campbell an actress (1865–1940);
Dr Crippin celebrated poisoner (1862–1910).

GEORGE	Where?
SARAH	The Duke of Westminster, I expect. It always is.
GEORGE	Ah, well, perhaps. To be or not to be. I don't know any more of it.

She looks irritated at him; then she coughs three times. He remembers and unzips her dress; she slaps him.

SARAH	Elyot, please. We are on our honeymoons.
GEORGE	Are we?
SARAH	Yes. *(irritated, being over-explicit)* Me with Victor, and you with Sibyl.
GEORGE	Ah.
SARAH	Tell me about Sibyl.
GEORGE	I've never met her.
SARAH	Ah, Elyot, you're so amusing. You're married to Sibyl. Tell me about her.
GEORGE	Nothing much to tell really. She's sort of nondescript, I'd say.
SARAH	I bet you were going to say that she's just like Lady Bundle, and that she has several chins, and one blue eye and one brown eye and a third eye in the center of her forehead. Weren't you?
GEORGE	Yes. I think so.
SARAH	Victor's like that too. *(Long pause.)* I bet you were just about to tell me that you traveled around the world.
GEORGE	Yes I was. I traveled around the world.
SARAH	How was it?
GEORGE	The world?

SARAH	Yes.
GEORGE	Oh, very nice.
SARAH	I always feared the Taj Mahal would look like a biscuit box. Did it?
GEORGE	Not really.

150

SARAH	*(she's going to give him the cue again)* I always feared the Taj Mahal would look like a biscuit box. Did it?
GEORGE	I guess it did.
SARAH	*(again)* I always feared the Taj Mahal would look like a biscuit box. Did it?

155

GEORGE	Hard to say. What brand biscuit box?
SARAH	I always feared the Taj Mahal would look like a biscuit box. Did it? *(Pause.)* Did it? Did it?
GEORGE	I wonder whose yacht that is out there.

160

SARAH	Did it? Did it? Did it? Did it?

Enter Meg. She's put on an apron and maid's hat and carries a duster, but is otherwise still in her stage manager's garb.

MEG	My, this balcony looks dusty. I think I'll just clean it up a little. *(Dusts and goes to George and whispers in his ear; exits.)*
GEORGE	Not only did the Taj Mahal look like a biscuit box, but women should be struck regularly like gongs. *(Applause.)*

165

SARAH	Extraordinary how potent cheap music is.
GEORGE	Yes. Quite extraordinary.
SARAH	How was China?
GEORGE	China?

170

SARAH	You traveled around the world. How was China?

GEORGE	I liked it, but I felt homesick.
SARAH	*(again this is happening; gives him cue again)* How was China?
GEORGE	Lots of rice. The women bind their feet.
SARAH	How was China?
GEORGE	I hated it. I missed . . . Sibyl.
SARAH	How was China?
GEORGE	I . . . miss the maid. Oh, maid!
SARAH	*How was China?*
GEORGE	Just wait a moment please. Oh, maid!

Enter Meg.

Ah, there you are. I think you missed a spot here.

She crosses, dusts, and whispers in his ear; exits.

SARAH	How was China?
GEORGE	*(with authority)* Very large, China.
SARAH	And Japan?
GEORGE	*(doesn' t know, but makes a guess)* Very . . . small, Japan.
SARAH	And Ireland?
GEORGE	Very . . . green.
SARAH	And Iceland?
GEORGE	Very white.
SARAH	And Italy?
GEORGE	Very . . . Neapolitan.
SARAH	And Copenhagen?
GEORGE	Very . . . cosmopolitan.
SARAH	And Florida?
GEORGE	Very condominium.

175

180

185

190

195

| SARAH | And **Perth Amboy**? | 200 |

SARAH And **Perth Amboy**?

GEORGE Very . . . mobile home, I don't know.

SARAH And Sibyl?

GEORGE What?

SARAH Do you love Sibyl?

GEORGE Who's Sibyl?

SARAH Your new wife, who you married after you and I got our divorce.

GEORGE Oh were we married? Oh yes, I forgot that part.

SARAH Elyot, you're so amusing. You make me laugh all the time. *(Laughs.)* So, do you love Sibyl?

GEORGE Probably. I married her.

Pause. She coughs three times, he unzips her dress, she slaps him.

SARAH Oh, Elyot, darling, I'm sorry. We were mad to have left each other. Kiss me.

They kiss. Enter Dame Ellen Terry as Sibyl, in an evening gown.

ELLEN Oh, how ghastly.

SARAH Oh dear. And this must be Sibyl.

ELLEN Oh how ghastly. What shall we do?

SARAH We must all speak in very low voices and attempt to be civilized.

ELLEN Is this Amanda? Oh, Elyot, I think she's simply obnoxious.

SARAH How very rude.

ELLEN Oh, Elyot, how can you treat me like this?

GEORGE Hello, Sibyl.

Perth Amboy small port town in New Jersey.

ELLEN	Well, since you ask, I'm very upset. I was inside writing a letter to your mother and wanted to know how to spell apothecary.	225
SARAH	A-P-O-T-H-E-C-A-R-Y.	
ELLEN	*(icy)* Thank you.	
	Writes it down; Sarah looks over her shoulder.	
SARAH	Don't scribble, Sibyl.	230
ELLEN	Did my eyes deceive me, or were you kissing my husband a moment ago?	
SARAH	We must all speak in very low voices and attempt to be civilized.	
ELLEN	I was speaking in a low voice.	235
SARAH	Yes, but I could still hear you.	
ELLEN	Oh. Sorry. *(Speaks too low to be heard)*	
SARAH	*(Speaks inaudibly also.)*	
ELLEN	*(Speaks inaudibly.)*	
SARAH	*(Speaks inaudibly.)*	240
ELLEN	*(Speaks inaudibly.)*	
SARAH	I can't hear a bloody word she's saying. The woman's a nincompoop. Say something, Elyot.	
GEORGE	I couldn't hear her either.	245
ELLEN	Elyot, you have to choose between us immediately – do you love this creature, or do you love me?	
GEORGE	I wonder where the maid is.	
ELLEN AND SARAH	*(together, furious)* Forget about the maid, Elyot!	250
	They look embarrassed.	
ELLEN	*(trying to cover)* You could never have a lasting	

relationship with a maid. Choose between the two of us.

GEORGE I choose . . . oh God, I don't know my lines. I don't know how I got here. I wish I *weren't* here. I wish I had joined the monastery like I almost did right after high school. I almost joined, but then I didn't. 25

SARAH *(trying to cover)* Oh, Elyot, your malaria is acting up again and you're ranting. Come, come, who do you choose, me or that baggage over there. 260

ELLEN You're the baggage, not I. Yes, Elyot, who do you choose?

GEORGE I choose . . . *(to Sarah)* I'm sorry, what is your name? 26

SARAH Amanda.

GEORGE I choose Amanda. I think that's what he does in the play.

ELLEN Very well. I can accept defeat gracefully. I don't think I'll send this letter to your mother. She has a loud voice and an overbearing manner and I don't like her taste in tea china. I hope, Elyot, that when you find me hanging from the hotel lobby chandelier with my eyes all bulged out and my tongue hanging out, that you'll be very, very sorry. Good-bye. *(Exits.)* 270 27

SARAH What a dreadful sport she is.

GEORGE *(doing his best to say something his character might)* Poor Sibyl. She's going to hang herself. 28

SARAH Some women should be hung regularly like tapestries. Oh who cares? Whose yacht do you think that is?

| GEORGE | *(remembering)* The Duke of Westminster, I exp . . . | 285 |

| SARAH | *(furious)* How dare you mention that time in Mozambique? *(Slaps him.)* Oh, darling. I'm sorry. *(moving her cigarette grandly)* I love you madly. |

| GEORGE | *(gasps)* I've inhaled your cigarette ash. | 290 |

He coughs three times. Sarah looks confused, then unzips the front of his Hamlet doublet. He looks confused, then slaps her. She slaps him back with a vengeance. They both look confused.

| SARAH | There, we're not angry anymore, are we? Oh, Elyot, wait for me here and I'll pack my things and we'll run away together before Victor gets back. Oh, darling, isn't it extraordinary how potent cheap music can be? | 295 |

She exits; recorded applause on her exit. George sort of follows a bit, but then turns back to face the audience. Flash photos are taken again; George blinks and is disoriented. Lights change, the sound of trumpets is heard, and Henry Irving, dressed in Shakespearean garb, enters and bows grandly to George.

| HENRY | Hail to your Lordship! |

| GEORGE | Oh hello. Are you Victor? |

| HENRY | The same, my Lord, and your poor servant ever. | 300 |

| GEORGE | This doesn't sound like Noël Coward. |

| HENRY | A truant disposition, good my Lord. |

| GEORGE | You're not Victor, are you? |

HENRY	My Lord, I came to see your father's funeral.
GEORGE	Oh yes? And how was it?
HENRY	Indeed, my Lord, it followed hard upon.
GEORGE	Hard upon? Yes, I see.

Enter Meg.

Oh, good, the maid.

She whispers to him.

Thrift, thrift, Horatio. The funeral baked meats did coldly furnish forth the marriage tables. What does that mean?

Meg exits.

Ah, she's gone already.

HENRY	My Lord, I think I saw him yesternight.
GEORGE	Did you? Who?
HENRY	My Lord, the king your father.
GEORGE	The king my father?
HENRY	Season your admiration for a while with an **attent** ear till I may deliver upon the witness of these gentlemen this marvel to you.
GEORGE	I see. I'm Hamlet now, right?
HENRY	Sssh! *(rattling this off in a very Shakespearean way)* Two nights together had these gentlemen, Marcellus and Bernardo, on their watch In the dead waste and middle of the night Been thus encountered. A figure like your father, Armed at point exactly, **cap a pe**,

305

310

315

320

325

---

attent attentive;
cap a pe from head to foot.

Appears before them and with solemn march
Goes slow and stately by them. Thrice he
    walked 330
By their oppressed and fear-surprised eyes
Within his truncheon's length, whilst they,
    distilled
Almost to jelly with the act of fear,
Stand dumb and speak not to him. This to me 335
In dreadful secrecy impart they did,
And I with them the third night kept the
    watch,
Where, as they had delivered, both in time,
Form of the thing, each word made true and 340
    good,
The apparition comes. I knew your father.
These hands are not more like.

GEORGE Oh, my turn? Most strange and wondrous
tale you tell, Horatio. It doth turn my ear 345
into a very . . . *(at a loss)* merry . . . bare **bodkin**.

HENRY As I do live, my honored lord, tis true,
and we did think it writ down in our duty
To let you know of it.

GEORGE Well, thank you very much. *(Pause.)* 350

HENRY Oh yes, my lord. He wore his **beaver** up.

GEORGE His beaver up. He wore his beaver up. And
does he usually wear it down?

HENRY A countenance more in sorrow than in
anger. 355

GEORGE Well I am sorry to hear that. My father was a
king of much renown. A favorite amongst all
in London town. *(Pause.)* And in Denmark.

---

bodkin a type of dagger;
beaver the face-guard of a suit of armour.

HENRY	I war'nt it will.
GEORGE	I war'nt it will also. 360
HENRY	Our duty to your honor. *(Exits.)*
GEORGE	Where are you going? Don't go.

Smiles out at audience. Enter Sarah dressed as Queen Gertrude.

GEORGE	Oh, Amanda, good to see you. Whose yacht do you think that is?
SARAH	Oh speak to me no more. 365 Thou turn'st mine eyes into my very soul, And there I see such black and grained spots As will not leave their **tinct**.
GEORGE	I haven't seen Victor. Someone was here who I thought might have been him, but it wasn't. 370
SARAH	O Hamlet, speak no more. These words like daggers enter in mine ears. No more, sweet Hamlet.
GEORGE	Very well. What do you want to talk about?
SARAH	No more! *(Exits.)* 375
GEORGE	Oh don't go. *(Pause. George smiles uncomfortably at the audience.)* Maybe someone else will come out in a minute. *(Pause.)* Of course sometimes people have soliloquies in Shakespeare. Let's just wait a moment more and maybe 380 someone will come.

The lights suddenly change to a dim blue background and one bright white spot center stage. George is not standing in the spot.

Oh dear. *(He moves somewhat awkwardly into the*

---

tinct colour.

spot, decides to do his best to live up to the requirements of the moment.) To be or not to be, that is the question. *(Doesn't know any more.)* Oh maid! *(No response; remembers that actors call for 'line'.)* Line! Line! Ohhhh. Oh, what a rogue and peasant slave am I. Whether tis nobler in the mind's eye to kill oneself, or not killing oneself, to sleep a great deal. We are such stuff as dreams are made on; and our lives are rounded by a little sleep. 385

390

The lights change. The spot goes out, and another one comes up stage right. George moves into it.

Uh, thrift, thrift, Horatio. Neither a borrower nor a lender be. But to thine own self be true. There is a special providence in the fall of a sparrow. Extraordinary how potent cheap music can be. Out, out, damn spot! I come **to wive it wealthily** in Padua; if wealthily, then happily in Padua. *(Sings.) Brush up your Shakespeare; start quoting him now; Da da . . .* 395

400

Lights change again. That spot goes off; another one comes on, center stage, though closer to audience. George moves into that.

I wonder whose yacht that is. How was China? Very large, China. How was Japan? Very small, Japan. I pledge allegiance to the flag of the United States of America and to the republic for which it stands, one nation, under God, indivisible with liberty and justice for all. Line! Line! Oh my God. *(Gets* 405

---

to wive it wealthily to find a wealthy woman to marry.

idea.) Oh my God, I am heartily sorry for having offended thee, and I detest all my sins because I dread the loss of heaven and the pains of hell. But most of all because they offend thee, my God, who art all good and deserving of all my love. And I resolve to confess my sins, to do penance, and to amend my life, Amen.

(friendly) That's the act of contrition that Catholic school children say in confession in order to be forgiven their sins. Catholic adults say it too, I imagine. I don't know any Catholic adults. Line!

(explaining) When you call for a line, the stage manager normally gives you your next line, to refresh your memory. Line! The quality of mercy is not strained. It droppeth as the gentle rain upon the place below, when we have shuffled off this mortal coil. Alas, poor Yorick. I knew him well. Get thee to a nunnery. Line.

Nunnery. As a child, I was taught by nuns, and then in high school I was taught by Benedictine priests. I really rather liked the nuns, they were sort of warm, though they were fairly crazy too. Line. I liked the priests also. The school was on the grounds of the monastery, any my junior and senior years I spent a few weekends joining in the daily routine of the monastery – prayers, then breakfast, then prayers, then lunch, then prayers, then dinner, then prayers, then sleep. I found the predictability quite attractive. And the food was good. I was going to join the

monastery after high school, but they said I
was too young and should wait. And then
I just stopped believing in all those things, so I
never did join the monastery. I became an   445
accountant. I've studied logarithms, and
cosine and tangent . . .

(irritated) LINE!

(apologetic) I'm sorry. This is supposed to be
Hamlet or *Private Lives* or something, and I   450
keep rattling on like a maniac. I really do
apologize. I just don't recall attending a
single rehearsal. I can't imagine what I was
doing. And also you came expecting to see
Edwin Booth and you get me. I really am   455
very embarrassed. Sorry. *Line!*

I have always depended on the kindness of
strangers. *Stella!* It is a far, far better thing I
do than I have ever done before. It's a far, far
better place I go to than I have ever been   460
before. *(sings the alphabet song)* a, b, c, d, e, f, g,
h, i, j, k, l, m, n, o, p, q, r, s, t . . .

*As he starts to sing, enter Ellen Terry, dragging two
large garbage cans. She puts them side by side, gets
in one.*

Oh, good. Are you Ophelia? Get thee to a
nunnery.

*She points to the other garbage can, indicating he
should get in it.*

Get in? Okay. *(He does.)* This must be one of   465
those modern *Hamlets*.

Lights change abruptly to stark 'Beckett lighting.'

ELLEN Nothing to be done. Pause. Pause. Wrinkle nose. *(Wrinkles nose.)* Nothing to be done.

GEORGE I guess you're not Ophelia. 470

ELLEN We'll just wait. Pause. Either he'll come, pause pause pause, or he won't.

GEORGE That's a reasonable attitude. Are we, on a guess, waiting for Godot?

ELLEN No, Willie. He came already and was an 475 awful bore. Yesterday he came. Garlic on his breath, telling a lot of unpleasant jokes about Jews and Polacks and stewardesses. He was just dreadful, pause, rolls her eyes upward. *(She rolls her eyes.)* 480

GEORGE Well, I am sorry to hear that. Pause. So who are we waiting for?

ELLEN We're waiting for Letty.

GEORGE Ah. And is he a political organizer or something, I seem to recall? 485

ELLEN Yes, dear, he is a political organizer. He's always coming around saying get involved, get off your behinds and organize, fight the system, do this, do that, uh, he's exhausting, he's worse than Jane Fonda. And he has 490 garlic breath just like Godot, I don't know which of them is worse, and I hope neither of them ever comes here again. Blinks left eye, blinks right eye, closes eyes, opens them. *(Does this.)* 495

GEORGE So we're really not waiting for anyone, are we?

ELLEN No, dear, we're not. It's just another happy day, pause, smile, pause, picks nit from head. *(Picks nit from head.)*

GEORGE	Do you smell something?	500
ELLEN	That's not your line. Willie doesn't have that many lines. *(louder)* Oh, Willie, how talkative you are this morning!	
GEORGE	There seems to be some sort of muck at the bottom of this garbage can.	505
ELLEN	Mustn't complain, Willie. There's muck at the bottom of everyone's garbage can. Count your blessings, Willie. I do. *(counts to herself, eyes closed)* One. Two. Three. Are you counting, Willie?	510
GEORGE	I guess so.	
ELLEN	I'm up to three. Three is my eyesight. *(Opens her eyes.)* Oh my God, I've gone blind. I can't see, Willie. Oh my God. Oh what a terrible day. Oh dear. Oh my. *(suddenly very cheerful again)* Oh well. Not so bad really. I only used my eyes occasionally. When I wanted to see something. But no more!	515
GEORGE	I really don't know this play at all.	
ELLEN	Count your blessings, Willie. Let me hear you count them.	520
GEORGE	Alright. One. Two. Three.That's my eyesight. Four. That's my hearing. Five, that's my . . . **Master Charge**. Six, that's . . .	
ELLEN	Did you say God, Willie?	525
GEORGE	No.	
ELLEN	Why did you leave the monastery, Willie? Was it the same reason I left the opera?	
GEORGE	I have no idea.	

Master Charge a credit card.

ELLEN   I left the opera bcause I couldn't sing. They   530
they were mad to have hired me. Certifiable. And
they were certified shortly afterward, the
entire staff. They reside now at the Rigoletto
Home for the Mentally Incapacitated. In
Turin. Pause. Tries to touch her nose with   535
her tongue. *(Does this.)*

VOICE   Ladies and gentlemen, may I have your
attention please?

ELLEN   Oh, Willie, listen. A voice. Perhaps there is a
God.   540

VOICE   At this evening's performance, the role of Sir
Thomas More, the man for all seasons,
normally played by Edwin Booth, will be
played by George Spelvin. The role of Lady
Alice, normally played by Sarah Bernhardt,   545
will be played by Sarah Siddons. The role of
Lady Margaret, normally played by **Eleanora
Duse**, will be read by the stage manager.
And at this evening's performance the
executioner will play himself.   550

GEORGE   What did he say?

ELLEN   The executioner will play himself.

GEORGE   What does he mean, the executioner will
play himself?

Lights change to Man for All Seasons *general
lighting. Enter Sarah as Lady Alice (Sir Thomas More's
wife), and Meg with a few costumed touches but
otherwise in her stage manager's garb and carrying a
script as Lady Margaret (Sir Thomas More's
daughter). Note: Though Meg starts by referring to*

Eleanora Duse   an Italian actress, renowned for her tragic roles (1858–1924).

her script, quite quickly it becomes clear that she
knows the lines and does her best to play
Sir Thomas' daughter with appropriate passion and
seriousness.

MEG   Oh father, why have they locked you up in   555
this dreadful dungeon, it's more than I can
bear.

SARAH   I've brought you a custard, Thomas.

MEG   Mother's brought you a custard, father.

GEORGE   Yes, thank you.   560

MEG   Oh father, if you don't give in to King Henry,
they're going to cut your head off.

SARAH   Aren't you going to eat the custard I brought
you, Thomas?

GEORGE   I'm not hungry, thank you.   565

Sudden alarming crash of cymbals, or something
similarly startling musically occurs. The Executioner
appears upstage. He is dressed as the traditional
headsman – the black mask, bare chest and arms, the
large ax. The more legitimately alarming he looks the
better. He can be played by the same actor who plays
*Henry Irving if his build and **demeanor** are*
appropriate. If not, it is possible to have a different
actor play this role.

GEORGE   Oh my God. I've got to get out of here.

MEG   He's over here. And he'll never give in to the
King.

GEORGE   No, no, I might. Quick, is this all about Anne
Boleyn and everything?   570

---

demeanor appearance, bearing.

MEG Yes, and you won't give in because you believe in the Catholic Church and the infallibility of the Pope and the everlasting life of the soul.

GEORGE I don't necessarily believe in any of that. *(to Executioner)* Oh, sir, there's been an error. I think it's fine if the King marries Anne Boleyn. I just want to wake up. 575

MEG Oh don't deny God, father, just to spare our feelings. Mother and I are willing to have you dead if it's a question of principle. 580

SARAH The first batch of custard didn't come out all that well, Thomas. This is the second batch. But it has a piece of hair in it, I think.

GEORGE Oh shut up about your custard, would you? I don't think the Pope is infallible at all. I think he's a normal man with normal capabilities who wears gold slippers. I thought about joining the monastery when I was younger, but I didn't do it. 585 590

ELLEN *(waking up from a brief doze)* Oh I was having such a pleasant dream, Willie. Go ahead, let him cut your head off, it'll be a nice change of pace.

The Executioner, who has been motionless, now moves. In a sudden gesture, he reveals the cutting block that waits for George's head. Note: In the Playwrights Horizons production, our set designer constructed a square furniture piece that doubled as a settee and/or small cocktail table during the Private Lives *section. However, when the Executioner kicked the top of it, the piece fell open, revealing itself to contain a bloodied cutting block.*

GEORGE   That blade looks very real to me. I want to   595
          wake up now. Or change plays. I wonder
          whose yacht that is out there.

          Sarah offers him the custard again.

GEORGE   *No, thank you!* A horse, a horse! My
          kingdom for a horse!

EXECUTIONER   Sir Thomas More, you have been found   600
          guilty of the charge of High Treason. The
          sentence of the court is that you be taken to
          the Tower of London, thence to the place of
          execution, and there your head shall be
          stricken from your body, and may God have   605
          mercy on your soul.

          Meg helps George out of the garbage can.

GEORGE   All this talk about God. All right, I'm sorry I
          didn't go to the monastery, maybe I should
          have, and I'm sorry I giggled during Mass in
          third grade, but I see no reason to be killed   610
          for it.

ELLEN   Nothing to be done. That's what I find so
          wonderful.

          Meg puts George's head on the block.

GEORGE   No!

EXECUTIONER   Do I understand you right? You wish to   615
          reverse your previous stand on King Henry's
          marriage to Anne and to deny the Bishop of
          Rome?

GEORGE   Yes, yes, God, yes. I could care less. Let him
          marry eight wives.   620

EXECUTIONER   That's a terrible legacy of cowardice for Sir
          Thomas More to leave behind.

GEORGE	I don't care.
EXECUTIONER	I'm going to ignore what you've said and cut your head off anyway, and then we'll all pretend you went to your death nobly. The Church needs its saints, and school children have got to have heroes to look up to, don't you all agree?
ELLEN	I agree. I know I need someone to look up to. Pause smile picks her nose. *(Does this.)*
GEORGE	Yes, yes, I can feel myself waking up now. The covers have fallen off the bed, and I'm cold, and I'm going to wake up s o that I can reach down and pull them up again.
EXECUTIONER	Sir Thomas, prepare to meet your death.
GEORGE	Be quiet. I am about to wake up.
EXECUTIONER	Sir Thomas, prepare to meet your death.
GEORGE	I'm awake!

Looks around him. Sarah offers him custard again.

	No, I'm not.
SARAH	He doesn't know his lines.
EXECUTIONER	Sir Thomas, prepare to meet your death.
GEORGE	Line! Line!
MEG	You turn to the Executioner and say: 'Friend, be not afraid of your office. You send me to God.'
GEORGE	I don't like that line. Give me another.
MEG	That's the line in the script, George. Say it.
GEORGE	I don't want to.
MEG	Say it.

625

630

635

640

645

650

ELLEN	Say it, Willie. It'll mean a lot to me and to generations of school children to come.
SARAH	O Hamlet, speak the speech, I pray you, trippingly on the tongue.	655
EXECUTIONER	Say it!
GEORGE	Friend, be not afraid of your office. You send me . . . Extraordinary how potent cheap music is.	660
MEG	That's not the line.
GEORGE	Women should be struck regularly like gongs.
MEG	George, say the line right.
GEORGE	They say you can never dream your own death, so I expect I'll wake up just as soon as he starts to bring the blade down. So perhaps I should get it over with.	665
MEG	Say the proper line, George.

George kneels down.

GEORGE	Friend, be not afraid of your office.	670

Executioner raises his ax.

ELLEN	Good-bye, Willie.
SARAH	Good-bye, Hamlet.
MEG	Good-bye, George.
EXECUTIONER	Good-bye, Sir Thomas.
GEORGE	You send me to God.	675

Executioner raises the ax to bring it down. Blackout.
Sound of the ax coming down.

EXECUTIONER	*(in darkness)* Behold the head of Sir Thomas More.
ELLEN	*(in darkness)* Oh I wish I weren't blind and could see that, Willie. Oh well, no matter. It's still been another happy day. Pause, smile, wrinkles nose, pause, picks nit from head, pause, pause, wiggles ears, all in darkness, utterly useless, no one can see her. She stares ahead. Count two. End of play.

680

Music plays. Maybe canned applause. Lights come up for curtain calls. The four take their bows (if Henry Irving doesn't play the Executioner, he comes out for his bow as well). Sarah and Ellen have fairly elaborate bows, perhaps receiving flowers from the Executioner. They gesture for George to take his bow, but he seems to be dead. They look disorientated and then bow again, and lights out. End.

Activities and ideas for rehearsing *The Actor's Nightmare*

The following can be done in any order.

1 Devise a scene called 'The Pupil's Nightmare', or 'The Teacher's Nightmare'.

2 Create an improvised scene about a situation where things keep going wrong but the central character keeps going – that is very important. It could be someone throwing a dinner party who is very keen to impress the guest or guests, or a live television programme where unexpected things happen.

3 The author parodies and quotes several real plays in *The Actor's Nightmare*. The audience doesn't have to know these plays well

(or at all) to enjoy the play, but it is useful for you to know which plays are referred to:

- *Hamlet* by William Shakespeare (c. 1600)
- *Private Lives* by Noël Coward (1930)
- *Happy Days* by Samuel Beckett (1961)
- *A Man For All Seasons* by Robert Bolt (1960).

Research or read these plays and then use the activities in Section A, particularly in A11: Emoting (pages 84–9), to give you ideas about how to perform these parts of *The Actor's Nightmare*. It is important to make it clear to the audience when they are watching the play and when they are watching the play-within-the-play.

4 Christopher Durang always writes notes to the actor. Consider the following when you are rehearsing the play:

Once George gets over his initial shock at the crazy dream-like situation, he becomes involved with a 'game' – he is trying to guess what might be the right thing to say next. When he makes a good guess, I think it's perfectly acceptable that he smiles and nods at the audience, as if to say to them 'I'm actually doing OK now, aren't I?'

It's important that all Ellen's 'pause, pause, wrinkle nose' sorts of lines are done with commitment as if they are appropriate lines. The idea that she is saying her stage directions aloud is not meant to be that she's making a mistake, it's meant to be that that's how this play is done in this dream.

5 Although the play is a comedy, don't fall into the trap of delivering the lines as if you were a stand up comic. All the characters are taking the situation they are in seriously. Playing the serious intentions makes the play more funny not less so. Use the activities in A5: Communicating (pages 19–22) and A6: Interacting (pages 22–31) to make sure that you are clear on what the characters want from each other.

B5: *Linda Her*
by Harry Kondoleon (1984)

Harry Kondoleon (1954–94) is practically unknown in the United Kingdom. In the United States, his seventeen plays were widely performed and won two Obies (the award for the best 'Off Broadway' play). Reading *Linda Her*, you might be reminded of some American sitcoms: the characters talk fast and wittily, the plot twists unexpectedly. Yet *Linda Her*, like all Harry Kondoleon's plays, uses comedy as a vehicle for dealing with serious and painful themes.

Linda Her is a play of contrasts. The dialogue is elegant but the sentiments expressed are brutally frank and often outrageously cruel. The stillness of four people, one more or less permanently asleep, in a bedroom on a humid summer night, contrasts with the emotional turbulence and turmoil that simmers just beneath the surface.

Cast

Carol
Matt
Janet
Hilary

Late summer, the middle of the night.

The bedroom of a summer house.

*Center there is a double bed, four pillows, tangled sheets and Matt, a man in boxer shorts sleeping face down, some sheet tangled about him. Sitting up is Carol in a shift-like nightgown. There is a white **comforter**, tangled, draped, half thrown at the end of the bed.*

comforter *N. American* – a warm quilt.

Upstage of the bed there is a table and on it a medium-large electrical fan with four steel petals spinning with a minimum of racket.

On either side of the slightly askew bed (it is placed almost diagonally) are two, tall, white, Greek columns.

Barefeet. Moonlight.

CAROL   Matt? Wake up, I can't sleep.

MATT   *(still half asleep, sitting up only slightly)* What's wrong?

CAROL   The girl you told me about. I can't stop thinking about her.

MATT   What girl?   5

CAROL   Linda Her. Tell me about her again.

MATT   We were children together. Moved away and something or other happened and now she's gone. Good night. *(His head falls down to sleep again.)*

CAROL   Who told you she died?   10

MATT   *(head still down)* Someone in the post office.

Slight pause.

CAROL   You're not sorry I invited Janet here, are you? We really don't have that much in common. Do you like her, Janet? Matt? Matt.

MATT   *(muffled voice)* What?   15

CAROL   Do you like Janet?

MATT   Yes.

CAROL   But she's no Linda Her. You said everyone loved her.

MATT   Don't tell me you're jealous of a girl I admired in kindergarten.   20

CAROL   Don't be an ass! *(Slight pause.)* It's just that I picture her so clearly. This very beautiful, bright girl, who

everyone likes, with her whole life ahead of her
and then one day many years later boom you find
out she doesn't exist anymore – isn't that scary? 25
Matt? *(Slight pause.)* Are you sick of me? I'm sick of
me. *(Slight pause.)* Matt, can we go home early? I
really can't stand it anymore. Let's go home or just
away. What do you say? Can we leave in the
morning? Matt. 30

MATT We only have a week left.

CAROL That's too much. Say we'll leave tomorrow. Hilary
wants to leave too I can tell. Matt? Matt? I'm afraid.
Matt.

Enter Janet, a woman in a knee-length white nightgown.

JANET Hi. 35

CAROL Janet.

JANET I felt so good I couldn't sleep.

CAROL I'm glad you're up. I couldn't either and I want to
talk and the log I married won't. Come sit by me.
Not too close, it's unearthly hot. 40

JANET It's not too bad.

CAROL And you're glad you came for the week?

JANET Entirely glad.

CAROL *(asking truly)* Do you hate anything, Janet, does
anything make you not glad? 45

JANET What?

CAROL Run away with me. I mean it! Remember in
junior high school when our fathers once
wouldn't let us stay out until one hundred
o'clock or whatever it was and we swore to run 50
away? We were going to leave our awful

existences behind and join high society. Or low society. Do you remember?

JANET I don't remember running away.

CAROL No, that's just it, we never did. Now's the time. I 55
feel it so urgently. We'll take your car and share the
driving. I have my passport with me. *(Slight pause.)*

JANET What did you think of the way I stuffed the
tomatoes?

CAROL Why are you ignoring me, don't you think I'm 60
serious? I'm dead serious, I assure you. I've been
thinking about that little girl who was the idol of
Matt's **elementary school** and now she's dead.

Slight pause.

JANET Run away where? From what? From whom? To go
do what? Leave Matt and Hilary? Is that what 65
you're saying, Carol? What time is it? – crazy-chit-
chat-time?

CAROL No, you don't remember running away, how could
you? I remember now. You were the one who
talked us out of going. 70

JANET You're really serious. How do you find the nerve to
sit two inches from your husband, a man who in
my opinion is the nicest guy on earth and talk of
running away from him?

CAROL He can't even hear me. See? Matt! Matt! *(She slaps* 75
his behind.)

MATT *(startled)* What?!

CAROL Matt, Janet wants to know what you thought of the
way she stuffed the tomatoes.

MATT The best ever.

---

elementary school primary school.

He falls back, face down, to sleep. Enter Hilary, also in sleep attire, barefoot, no more than ten years old. She combs her own hair repetitiously, tirelessly.

CAROL Oh Hilary, hurray, you're here too! – and you've 80
brought your comb. Couldn't you sleep? Do you
see, Hilary knows there is no peace in this world.
And Hilary, if you're going to stand there getting
the benefits of the fan stand slightly to one side so
Janet and I can feel it too. 85

JANET I'm fine.

CAROL That's right, I keep forgetting. Hilary, wake up your
father and tell him you want to go back a week
early.

HILARY No. 90

CAROL Hilary, a little girl has died, a little girl has grown
up and died.

JANET Carol, have you lost your mind?! To talk to a child
that way!

CAROL You underrate Hilary, Janet, I promise you. Hilary 95
understands mortality better than you or I, don't
you, Hilary?

JANET I don't recognize you.

CAROL No, you don't. You don't recognize me because
you don't really know me. 100

JANET That's a *very* peculiar thing to say to a person who's
been your best friend since the **seventh grade**!

CAROL Do you remember how we became friends, Janet?
You brought me sandwiches. Everyday. I thought
to myself, why is this girl bringing me sandwiches? 105
Well, maybe she's a lesbian, that's cool.

---

seventh grade Year 8.

Hilary laughs briefly.

JANET Carol!

CAROL I didn't know yet that that was your method for everything, courtship by nourishment. Even this week you've worked so hard to make yourself 110 indispensable – is that what you do at your office, it's a wonder they can stand you – why doesn't this woman just give herself a vacation I thought to myself!

JANET Hilary, go back to your room and I'll make you a 115 paper fan you can use in bed and I'll bring it to you.

CAROL Hilary's not going anywhere. Once she finds a spot she like she sticks to it like a curse.

JANET So why are we friends, Carol?

CAROL I've asked myself that. 120

JANET Why then the phone calls every second or third week? You call me.

CAROL Well, the way I see it, it gets harder and harder to get rid of things, to just get rid of them. Take this summer cottage for example in the middle of 125 nowhere with **outlets** that don't work – why won't Matt just sell it? Hilary hates it, don't you, Hills? Why? – because Matty was a *boy* here, running back and forth and in circles and it all brings back memories or something and that as we get older I suppose is 130 enough reason not to throw something away.

JANET And I remind you of your girlhood.

CAROL I thought you did but sitting here now, in this light, I must say you remind me of nothing or, worse maybe still, of myself without hope. 135

---

outlets electrical sockets.

JANET Hope for what? – I'm not sure I want to know – I'm more interested in why this summer you bothered to invite me for a whole week – wasn't your conscience or curiosity free after a ten-minute call? 140

CAROL The truth? You started complaining about not having a man-friend or being married or having a child and I felt sorry for you – I did, I'm not saying this maliciously, I felt so sorry for you, you made your life sound so pitiful. 145

JANET Well, thank you very, very much!

CAROL So I thought I'd invite you out here and you'd have a great time and the really odd thing is you have. You have had nothing but fun. You've gotten along with Matt whose idea of a vacation is 150 uninterrupted sleep and even with Miss Hilary of the Damned. It's remarkable how well you've fit in.

JANET You're exaggerating to make me feel self-conscious, your **specialty**, I might say since we're taking this time to be so honest. 155

CAROL Right. Hilary, tell me what you think of Janet, evaluate her for us. Come on, don't be shy. Hilary is at the top of her class. She reads faster than anyone you or I have ever met and, more impressive still, she can sum up the book – any 160 book – in two or three sentences. Hilary, evaluate Janet.

HILARY *(no enthusiasm, matter-of-fact)* She keeps her room tidy and makes her bed right after getting out of it. She pushes her food with a small chunk of bread which 165 she eats at the end of every meal. She doesn't like sweets but doesn't frown on those who do.

---

specialty speciality (American).

CAROL	More.
HILARY	Her cookies which she says she made up the recipe to are the best I've ever eaten. 170
CAROL	Bravo! *(to Janet)* There, you see?
JANET	It's none of my business but if you were nicer to her I think she would respond to you more.
CAROL	Oh, Janet, you're so dense, you don't read anything for what it is, you're always on the wrong 175 page or something. Hilary, tell Janet what you think of me. Go on, tell her.
HILARY	*(after a pause)* You're not a phony.
CAROL	You see, there it is. Hilary is a sort of fortune cookie in reverse. *I'm not a phony*. Well, thank 180 you, Hilary, but did you know how sometimes, more than anything, I just wish I were a phony, just one big phony, and then all my problems would be solved!
JANET	I think you should go to sleep. 185
CAROL	I can't sleep. Isn't that obvious, Janet? I cannot sleep and I cannot rest or relax or take my mind off *X*, *Y* or *Z* and now, in the middle of all *this*, I am confronted with *her*.
JANET	Who? 190
CAROL	Her. *Her*. Linda Her.
JANET	The girl who died? What, mortality? – everyone's going to die one day. To dwell on it, Carol, is just downbeat.
CAROL	Naturally. Hilary, say something upbeat about 195 mortality to cheer us up.
HILARY	At the science fair in school Mrs Hoffman fell down the stairs and had to get a cast on her foot so now when she goes up or down steps she counts them out loud. 200

| CAROL | I can always depend on Hilary for the good news. How vividly I see Mrs Hoffman taking her fall and from that day on counting her every step. Mrs Hoffman must know that life is a slippery stairwell. |

| JANET | I can be gratuitously morbid too and say that there's nothing ahead of us but repetitions of old bad days but I wouldn't believe it! |

| CAROL | I would. |

| JANET | Well then I have no hope for you! No hope and no kind words! |

| CAROL | Thank you, that's what I thought. Why don't you stay here, Janet? |

| JANET | What? |

| CAROL | You understood exactly what I meant. Stay here with Matt and Hilary. |

| JANET | The week? |

| CAROL | Forever. Forever and ever and then a week after that. For good. |

| JANET | I'm going back to my room. |

| CAROL | No – stay here and I'll leave. |

| JANET | Hilary, go to your bed. |

| HILARY | No. |

| CAROL | Hilary combs her hair like that all day to hypnotize herself into a state of conformity so she can *excel* and when she graduates from business school her real personality will pop out and she'll bite the heads off of executives like so many chicken heads, won't you, Hilary? |

| HILARY | Maybe. |

| JANET | Would you like me to call a doctor? |

| CAROL | Not unless you feel sick. Do you see, Janet, this is |

your chance of a lifetime, take it. You say you haven't the knack of meeting men and that family life is both alluring and elusive; here it is, table set. You don't mind Hilary – she's really no less friendly to you than anyone else. My theory on why there are children is so that the minute you finish growing up – you know, that whole period where you feel excluded from everything, they show up to exclude you again. 235

240

JANET Is it possible you've become so hard-hearted as to say such horrific things in front of a child!

CAROL First of all, Janet, and you know this as well as I do, Hilary is Matt's child, not mine. And as far as the horrific goes with Hilary I couldn't hope to 245 compete. Tell Janet, Hilary, what you told me, tell her. *(Slight pause.)* I order you to tell her!

HILARY I think how I have to work very hard in school and get excellent grades so I can become very powerful one day and punish all the people who 250 ever bothered me.

CAROL She saw on one of those talk shows that are on all day a woman who used to be some kind of movie star and became a make-up tycoon and said her whole motivation in life was getting back at people 255 who had mistreated her as a child. So you see, Janet, Hilary's someone you can really work with – and she loves your sandwiches.

JANET Who's bothered you, Hilary, tell me.

CAROL And you do like Matt, you have a **real rapport** with 260 him, admit it. Admit it. Admit it, Janet.

JANET It's true I find his work interesting.

---

real rapport very good relationship.

CAROL   Interesting? I have often thought it would be more
interesting to be dead than to do what Matt does
but he gets paid so much I feel like a hypocrite   265
when I put it down.

JANET   You shouldn't do that.

CAROL   I agree with you but I can't help it and he says he
doesn't mind but deep down of course he must.

JANET   He's not attracted to me.   270

CAROL   I don't think it matters a damn anymore,
attraction. It's something you see beyond or into
or impose an image on or you just get to a place
where you're past caring.

JANET   It's no surprise you're depressed, Carol, when you   275
reduce everything down like that. I may be
pathetic but I'm not dead. There's something dead
about you.

CAROL   Yes, I know. I'm sure I'd be happier if I could find a
plainer more adaptable self, someone more like   280
you, Janet.

JANET   Even if I were to stay here while you took a vacation
– a vacation from I-don't-know-what since your life
has always resembled a vacation to me – even if I
were to consider something so crazy, how would –   285

CAROL   You're not getting me, Janet. Listen then to Matt.
(She shakes Matt awake.) Matt, what do I always say
about Janet?

MATT   Nothing.

CAROL   There it is, Janet, from the mouth of sleep: I say   290
nothing about you. When we're not talking on the
telephone you don't exist for me – why should I
for you? Stay here the week and then move into
the apartment after that. Cut what dresses you

don't like hanging in the closet into square pieces 295
and use them to dust – you like to dust – dust with
them.

JANET In the ninth grade, because it suited your self-
image as editor to have some underling there to
underline everything you had to say, you let me on 300
the literary magazine even though I couldn't write
or draw. But guess what, Carol? You couldn't write
or draw either.

CAROL That's so true. But you were such a blank, Janet,
when I stood next to you I felt exciting and 305
complicated. Now you know.

JANET In other words you'd take off, just like that.

CAROL In other words, yes.

JANET And what about me? I'm supposed to just leave
my life behind as if it were a . . . footprint or 310
something?

CAROL What will you be leaving behind? Your telephone?
You already know my number. Now it's yours. You
like to stuff tomatoes, Janet, stuff tomatoes,
peppers, **eggplants**, the empty pots on the porch, 315
the car, the twelve months of the year, stuff
everything.

JANET Very funny. You've always made me feel a little bit
tatty and out-of-the-joke, haven't you?

CAROL Yes. 320

JANET And you haven't been a very good friend to me,
really at all, after all.

CAROL No, I suppose I haven't, I'm sorry.

JANET So, what now?

---

eggplants aubergines (American).

CAROL	I'll open the door and walk outside of it.	325
JANET	In your nightgown?	
CAROL	Probably. I'll walk along the road until a car passes and picks me up and maybe not the first car or the second car but surely by the third one I'll have found a new life, another ready-made, maybe, and I'll drive to that.	330
JANET	Is this all because of that little girl, Linda?	
CAROL	I don't feel sorry for her. When you're a star like that in kindergarten there's no place left to climb. Hilary, do you want to say something to me? *(Slight pause.)*	335
JANET	What should I tell Matt?	
CAROL	Tell him the place we had lunch today used pancake batter as salad dressing. Tell him I'm looking for a good restaurant. Tell him I've dyed my hair and gone back to kindergarten. Tell him I couldn't sleep. Good bye. *(Carol exits. Hilary, frightened, cries, Matt wakes up.)*	340
MATT	Are you crying, Hilary?	
HILARY	No.	
MATT	I didn't think so, not such a smart girl like you. Can't you sleep, sweetheart? Come sit by me and I'll tell you a little story.	345
HILARY	A scary one?	
MATT	When I was your age, Hilary, and in school, there was a little girl named Linda Her and she was the prettiest girl in the whole school.	350
HILARY	Like me.	
MATT	Yes, Hilary, as pretty as you. And she was the smartest too.	

HILARY	But not smarter than me.	355
MATT	No. And whenever a little boy had a birthday party he would invite Linda even though these parties were for all boys and she would be the only girl because she was so popular.	
HILARY	Then what happened?	360
MATT	Well, then, my mother – your grandma – moved away and I went to another school and then I went away to yet another school where I met your Mommy and then lots of other things happened and here we are.	365
HILARY	And Linda?	
MATT	She died just like everyone's going to die one day, only sooner. Now, Hilary, that's not a scary story, is it?	
HILARY	Mrs Hoffman at the science fair said that it's cold on the moon.	370
MATT	When you're an old woman, Hilary, you're going to think back and ask yourself why couldn't I let my father sleep.	
HILARY	But I'm afraid.	
MATT	I've told you there's nothing to be afraid of. Now just put your head on the pillow and close your eyes and then you'll be asleep. Janet, what are you doing there?	375
JANET	Nothing, just thinking.	

Activities and ideas for rehearsing *Linda Her*

The following can be done in any order.

1   There is a fourth wall between the audience and the actors in *Linda Her*, but that does not mean to say that the play is naturalistic. The fact that the conversation is heightened and stylised means that the actors need to find and understand the intentions and emotions which underpin the characters' actions. So the activities in A11: Emoting (on intensification, pages 88–9), A4: Connecting (pages 15–19) and A5: Communicating (pages 19–22) are particularly useful when rehearsing *Linda Her*.

2   Improvise some scenes that take place before the play begins, to help you create the characters' histories. Write biographies for all the characters, based on what you have imagined and decided in the activities above.

   It will also be helpful to use the questions on the characters' situations in B1: Overview of the Rehearsal Process (page 93) to help you decide about particular moments in the play, for instance:

   • For Carol, is leaving a new idea that arises from the conversation she has with Janet, or is it something she has been thinking about for some time?
   • Why does Hilary cry?
   • Does Hilary like Carol?

3   To establish the style of the piece, try running through the play in the following ways as part of your rehearsal process:

   • The play is set on a humid night. Perform as if your character begins in a bad mood because every movement is an effort and causes you to sweat.
   • Each character stands at the corner of a large square. Make the distance between the characters as big as possible. You cannot move from your corner but you can face towards or away from the character addressing you, depending on the impact of what is being said. Make sure you speak loudly and clearly.

- Stage the play as if it was a knock down, no-holds-barred quarrel.
- Run through the play with the characters sitting as close as possible to each other – uncomfortably close, even. Whisper the lines to each other.

Discuss what the group discovered when running *Linda Her* in the four different ways described. Which of those discoveries will you use in your final performance, and why?

B6: *Story In Harlem Slang* from *Spunk: 3 Tales* by George C Wolfe (1989)

This play is based on a story written in 1942 by Zora Neale Hurston (1903–60), who was a novelist, playwright and historian. She was part of the Harlem Renaissance, a group of African American writers, artists and musicians in the 1920s and 1930s who believed that African Americans could not achieve social equality by emulating white ideals and that equality could only be achieved by teaching racial pride with an emphasis on an African cultural heritage.

Story in Harlem Slang was written in 1942 but the stage adaptation was first performed in 1989, along with *Sweat* and *The Gilded Six Bits*. (Incidentally, 'spunk' is American slang for spirit or courage.) Zora Neale Hurston's work was and still is controversial because she did not shy away from negative – some might say stereotypical – images – of African Americans. It is useful to compare *Story in Harlem Slang* with *Bouncers* (pages 5–10), which explores and uses stereotypes from a different place and time. It is also useful, when reading the play, to think about whether white actors can or should perform the play. How would casting white actors affect the images of and messages about African American experience?

George C Wolfe is an African American director, playwright and composer. His work explores and re-evaluates African American culture. *Story In Harlem Slang* uses 1940s street talk and movement and physicalisation based on urban dance styles. This is emphasised by the way music, scat-singing and rhythm underscore and punctuate the action. Characters move between narration and interaction.

George C Wolfe wrote the following note:

> It is suggested that the rhythms of the dialect be played, instead of the dialect itself. A subtle but important distinction. The former will give you Zora. The latter Amos and Andy [Amos and Andy were two white comedians, working from the 1930s until the early 1960s. They were part of the minstrel tradition where white performers 'blacked up' to present caricatures of African-American people as lazy, foolish and lovable].

Cast

Slang Talk Man
Jelly
Footnote Voice
Sweet Back
Girl
Blues Speak Woman
Guitar Man

The same person can play the parts of Footnote Voice and Girl. If you want to retain live music, use the rehearsal process to decide the best way of dividing up the parts of Blues Speak Women and Guitar Man.

The play can be performed by one female and three male performers but it also works when performed by four boys, because Girl is so much a stereotypical male fantasy creation – at least, at first!

> *Lights reveal Slang Talk Man: his attire, very **debonair**; his manner of speaking, very smooth.*

debonair pleasant and affable.

SLANG TALK MAN	Wait till I light up my coal-pot and tell you about this **Zigaboo** called **Jelly**.

*On Slang Talk Man's signal, lights reveal Jelly, a **hick** trying to pass himself off as slick. He wears a stocking cap and underneath his 'street' bravado is a boyish charm.*

JELLY	Well all right now!
SLANG TALK MAN	He was sealskin brown and papa-tree-top tall.
JELLY	Skinny in the hips and **solid** built for speed.
SLANG TALK MAN	He was born with this rough-dried hair, but when he laid on the grease and pressed it down overnight with his stocking-cap . . .

Jelly pulls off the cap to admire his 'do'.

JELLY	It looked just like **righteous moss**.
SLANG TALK MAN	Had so many waves, you got seasick from lookin'.
JELLY	Solid man solid.
SLANG TALK MAN	His mama named him Marvel, but after a month on Lenox Avenue . . .

On Slang Talk Man's signal, a zoot-suit jacket and hat magically appear.

SLANG TALK MAN	He changed all that to –
JELLY	*(getting dressed)* Jelly.

Zigaboo an African American; **Jelly** a nickname meaning 'Sexy Guy';
hick unsophisticated person from out of town; **solid** perfect;
righteous moss good hair.

| SLANG TALK MAN | How come? Well he put it in the street that when it comes to filling that long-felt need . . . | 20 |

| JELLY | Sugar-curing the ladies' feelings . . . | |

| SLANG TALK MAN | He was in a class by himself. And nobody knew his name, so he had to tell 'em. | 25 |

| JELLY | It must be Jelly cause jam don't shake! | |

| SLANG TALK MAN | That was what was on his sign. The stuff was there and it was mellow. N' whenever he was challenged by a hard-head or a **frail eel** on the right of his title, he would eyeball the idol-breaker with a slice of ice and say – | 30 |

| JELLY | **Youse just dumb to the fact**, baby. If you don't know what you talking 'bout, you better ask **Granny Grunt**. I wouldn't mislead you baby. I don't need to. Not with the help I got. | 35 |

| SLANG TALK MAN | Then he would give the pimp's sign . . . | 40 |

Jelly and Slang Talk Man adopt an exaggerated 'street' pose; for Slang Talk Man it's empty posturing; for Jelly it's the real deal.

And percolate on down the Avenue.

On Slang Talk Man's signal, the Footnote Voice is heard. As the Voice speaks, Jelly practices a series of poses.

---

frail eel pretty girl;
Youse just dumb to the fact you don't know what you're talking about;
Granny Grunt a mythical character to whom most questions may be referred.

| FOOTNOTE VOICE | Please note. In Harlemese, pimp has a different meaning than its ordinary definition. The Harlem pimp is a man whose **amatory talents** are for sale to any woman who will support him, either with a free meal or on a **common-law basis**; in this sense, he is actually a male prostitute. | 45 |

| SLANG TALK MAN | So this day he was **airing out** on the Avenue. It had to be late afternoon, or he would not have been out of bed. | 50 |

| JELLY | Shoot, all you did by rolling out early was to stir your stomach up. *(confidentially)* That made you hunt for more **dishes to dirty**. The longer you slept, the less you had to eat. | 55 |

| SLANG TALK MAN | But you can't **collar nods** all day. So Jelly . . . |

Music underscore.

Got into his **zoot suit with the reet pleats** and got out to skivver around and do himself some good. 60

The transformation from 'Jelly the Hick' into 'Jelly the Slick' is now complete. He struts and poses like a tiger on the prowl; his moves suggestive, arrogant, mocking.

---

amatory talents skill or talent in love-making;
common-law basis unmarried but living like husband and wife;
airing out leaving, fleeing, strolling; **dishes to dirty** to eat; **collar nods** sleep;
zoot suit with the reet pleats Harlem-style suit with padded shoulders, 43-inch trousers at the knee with turn-up so small it needs a zipper to get into, high waistline, fancy lapels, bushels of buttons, etc.

Lights reveal Blues Speak Woman and Guitar Man, sitting outside the playing arena, scatting vocalise which accents Jelly's moves.

JELLY   No matter how long you stay in bed, and how quiet you keep, sooner or later that big guts is going to reach 65 over and grab that little one and start to gnaw. That's confidential from the Bible. You got to get out on the beat and collar yourself a hot!

SLANG TALK MAN   At 132nd Street, he spied one of his 70 colleagues, Sweet Back! Standing on the opposite sidewalk, in front of a café.

Lights reveal Sweet Back, older than Jelly; the wear and tear of the street is starting to reveal itself in Sweet Back's face.

Nonetheless, he moves with complete finesse as he and Jelly stalk each other, each trying to outdo the other as they strut, pose and lean.

Jelly figured that if he **bull-skated** just right, he might **confidence** Sweet 75 Back out of a **thousand on a plate**. Maybe a shot of **scrap-iron** or a **reefer**. Therefore, they both took a quick backward look at the soles of their shoes to see how their leather was 80 holding out. They then **stanched out** into the street and made the crossing.

---

bull-skated bragged; **confidence** con; **thousand on a plate** beans (i.e. dinner); **scrap-iron** cheap liquor; **reefer** a marijuana cigarette, also a drag; **stanched out** stepped out.

Music underscore ends.

JELLY   Hey there, Sweet Back. **Gimme some skin!**

SWEET BACK   **Lay the skin on me** pal. Ain't seen 85
you since the last time, Jelly. What's
cookin'?

JELLY   Oh, just like the **bear**, I ain't no
where. Like the bear's brother, I ain't
no further. Like the bear's daughter, 90
ain't got a quarter.

SLANG TALK MAN   Right away he wished he had not
been so honest. Sweet Back gave
him a –

SWEET BACK   Top-superior, cut-eye look. 95

SLANG TALK MAN   Looked at Jelly just like –

SWEET BACK   A showman looks at an ape.

SLANG TALK MAN   Just as far above Jelly as fried chicken
is over **branch water**.

SWEET BACK   Cold in the hand huh? A red hot 100
pimp like you say you is ain't got no
business in the barrel. Last night
when I left you, you was **beating up
your gums** and broadcasting about
how hot you was. Just as hot as **July** 105
jam, you told me. What you doin'
cold in hand?

JELLY   Aw man, can't you take a joke? I was
just beating up my gums when I said
I was broke. How can I be broke 110

Gimme some skin! shake my hand!; **Lay the skin on me** shake hands;
bear 'the bear' is a confession of poverty; **branch water** fresh or pure water;
beating up your gums talking to no purpose; **July jam** something very hot.

	when I got the best woman in Harlem? If I ask her for a dime, she'll give me a ten dollar bill. Ask her for a drink of likker, and she'll buy me a whiskey still. If I'm lyin' I'm flyin'!	115
SWEET BACK	Man, don't hang out that dirty washing in my back yard. Didn't I see you last night with that beat chick, scoffing a hot dog? That chick you had was beat to the heels. Boy, you ain't no good for what you live. And you ain't got nickel one. *(as if to a passing woman)* Hey baby!	120
SLANG TALK MAN	Jelly –	
JELLY	Threw back the long skirt of his coat.	125
SLANG TALK MAN	And rammed his hand into his pants pocket. Sweet Back –	
SWEET BACK	Made the same gesture. . .	
SLANG TALK MAN	Of hauling out non-existent money.	
JELLY	Put your money where your mouth is. Back yo' crap with your money. I bet you five dollars.	130
SWEET BACK	Oh yeah!	
JELLY	Yeah.	

Jelly and Sweet Back move toward each other, wagging their pants pockets at each other.

| | | |
| **SWEET BACK** | *(playfully)* Jelly-Jelly-Jelly. I been raised in the church. I don't bet. But I'll doubt you. Five **rocks**! | 135 |

---

rocks dollars.

JELLY	I thought so. *(loud talking)* I knowed he'd back up when I **drawed my roll** on him.
	140
SWEET BACK	You ain't drawed no roll on me, Jelly. You ain't drawed nothing but your pocket. *(with an edge)* You better stop that boogerbooing. Next time I'm liable to make you do it.
	145
SLANG TALK MAN	There was a splinter of regret in Sweet Back's voice. If Jelly really had had some money, he might have staked him to a hot.
SWEET BACK	Good Southern cornbread with **a piano** on a platter.
	150
SLANG TALK MAN	Oh well! The right broad would . . . might come along.
JELLY	Who boogerbooing? **Jig,** I don't have to. Talkin' about me with a beat chick scoffing a hot dog? Man you musta not seen me, 'cause last night I was riding 'round in a Yellow Cab, with a yellow gal, drinking yellow likker and spending yellow money. *(to the audience)* Tell 'em 'bout me. You was there. Tell 'em!
	155
	160
SWEET BACK	Git out of my face Jelly! That broad I seen you with wasn't no **pe-ola**. She was one of them **coal-scuttle blondes** with hair just as close to her
	165

---

drawed my roll took out my roll of money;
a piano spare ribs (white rib bones suggest piano keys);
jig African American, a corrupted shortening of Zigaboo;
pe-ola a very white African American girl; **coal-scuttle blondes** black women.

head as ninety-nine to hundred. She
look-ted like she had seventy-five
pounds of clear bosom, and she look-
ted like six months in front and nine   170
months behind. Buy you a whiskey
still! That broad couldn't make the
down payment on a pair of sox.

JELLY   Naw-naw-naw-now Sweet Back, long
as you been knowing me, you ain't   175
never seen me with nothing but
pe-olas. I can get any frail eel I wants
to. How come I'm up here in New
York? Huh-huh-huh? You don't
know, do you? Since youse dumb to   180
the fact, I reckon I'll have to make
you hep. I had to leave from down
south cause **Miss Anne** used to
worry me so bad to go with her. Who
me? Man, **I don't deal in no coal**.   185

SWEET BACK   Aww man, you trying to show your
grandma how to milk ducks. Best you
can do is confidence some **kitchen-
mechanic** out of a dime or two. Me,
I knocks the pad with them   190
cackbroads up on **Sugar Hill** and fills
'em full of melody. Man, I'm quick
death 'n' easy judgment. You just a
home-boy, Jelly. Don't try to follow me.

Miss Anne a white woman;
I don't deal in no coal I don't keep company with black women;
kitchen-mechanic a domestic servant;
Sugar Hill part of Harlem and site of the newest apartment houses, mostly
occupied by professional people.

JELLY	Me follow you! Man, I come on like the Gang Busters and go off like The March of Time. If that ain't so, God is gone to Jersey City and you know He wouldn't be messing 'round a place like that.

195
200

SLANG TALK MAN	Looka there!

Sweet Back and Jelly scurry and look.

Oh well, the right broad might come along.

JELLY	Know what my woman done? We hauled off and went to church last Sunday. And when they passed 'round the plate for the penny collection, I throwed in a dollar. The man looked at me real hard for that. That made my woman mad, so she called him back and threwed in a twenty dollar bill. Told him to take that and go! That's what he got for looking at me 'cause I throwed in a dollar.

205
210

SWEET BACK	Jelly . . .

215

The wind may blow
And the door may slam
That what you shooting
Ain't worth a damn!

JELLY	Sweet Back you fixing to talk out of place.

220

SWEET BACK	If you tryin' to **jump salty** Jelly, that's yo' mammy.

---

jump salty get angry.

| JELLY | Don't play in the family Sweet Back. I don't **play the dozens**. I done told you. | 225 |

| SLANG TALK MAN | Jelly – |

| JELLY | Slammed his hand in his bosom as if to draw a gun. |

| SLANG TALK MAN | Sweet Back – | 230 |

| SWEET BACK | Did the same. |

| JELLY | If you wants to fight, Sweet Back, the favor is in me. |

Jelly and Sweet Back begin to circle one another, each waiting on the other to 'strike' first.

| SWEET BACK | I was deep-thinking then, Jelly. It's a good thing I ain't short-tempered. Tain't nothing to you nohow. | 235 |

| JELLY | Oh yeah. Well, come on. |

| SWEET BACK | No you come on. |

| SWEET BACK AND JELLY | *(overlapping)* Come on! Come on! Come on! Come on! | 240 |

They are now in each other's face, grimacing, snarling, ready to fight, when Sweet Back throws Jelly a look.

| SWEET BACK | You ain't hit me yet. |

They both begin to laugh, which grows, until they are falling all over each other: the best of friends.

Don't get too yaller on me Jelly. You liable to get hurt some day.

---

play the dozens insult an opponent's ancestors.

JELLY	You over-sports your hand yo' ownself. Too blamed **astorperious**. I just don't pay you no mind. Lay the skin on me man.
SLANG TALK MAN	They broke their handshake hurriedly, because both of them looked up the Avenue and saw the same thing.
SWEET BACK AND JELLY	It was a girl.
	Music underscore as lights reveal the girl, busily posing and preening.
SLANG TALK MAN	And they both remembered that it was Wednesday afternoon. All the domestics off for the afternoon with their pay in their pockets.
SWEET BACK AND JELLY	Some of them bound to be hungry for love.
SLANG TALK MAN	That meant . . .
SWEET BACK	Dinner!
JELLY	A shot of scrap-iron!
SWEET BACK	Maybe room rent!
JELLY	A reefer or two!
SLANG TALK MAN	They both . . .
SWEET BACK	Went into the pose.
JELLY	And put on the look. *(loud talking)* Big stars falling.
SLANG TALK MAN	Jelly said out loud when the girl was in hearing distance.
JELLY	It must be just before day!

245

250

255

260

265

270

---

astorperious haughty.

SWEET BACK	Yeah man. Must be recess in Heaven, pretty angel like that out on the ground.
SLANG TALK MAN	The girl drew abreast of them, reeling and rocking her hips.

Blues Speak Woman scats as the girl struts, her hips working to the beat of the music. Jelly and Sweet Back swoop in and begin their moves.

JELLY	I'd walk clear to **Diddy-Wah-Diddy** to get a chance to speak to a pretty li'l ground-angel like that.
SWEET BACK	Aw, man you ain't willing to go very far. Me, I'd go slap to **Ginny-Gall**, where they eat cow-rump, skin and all.
SLANG TALK MAN	The girl smiled, so Jelly set his hat and took the plunge.
JELLY	Ba-by, **what's on de rail for de lizard**?
SLANG TALK MAN	The girl halted and braced her hips with her hands.

Music underscore stops.

GIRL	A Zigaboo down in **Georgy**, where I come from, asked a woman that one time and the judge told him ninety days.

Music underscore continues.

Diddy-Wah-Diddy (1) a far place, a measure of distance; (2) a suburb of Hell;
Ginny-Gall another suburb of Hell, a long way off;
what's on de rail for de lizard? a sexual advance; **Georgy** Georgia.

SWEET BACK	Georgy! Where 'bouts in Georgy you from? Delaware?
JELLY	Delaware? **My people! My people!** Man, how you going to put Delaware 295 in Georgy. You ought to know that's in Maryland.

Music underscore stops.

GIRL	Oh, don't try to make out youse no northerner, you! Youse from right **down in 'Bam** your ownself. 300
JELLY	Yeah, I'm *from* there and I aims to stay from there.
GIRL	One of them **Russians**, eh? Rushed up here to get away from a job of work.

Music underscore continues.

SLANG TALK MAN	That kind of talk was not leading 305 towards the dinner table.
JELLY	But baby! That shape you got on you! I bet the Coca-Cola company is paying you good money for the patent!
SLANG TALK MAN	The girl smiled with pleasure at this, 310 so Sweet Back jumped in.
SWEET BACK	I know youse somebody swell to know. Youse real people. There's **dickty** jigs 'round here tries to smile. You grins like a regular fellow. 315

My people! My people! an African American expression used either sadly (a comment on the backwardness of some African Americans) or satirically; **down in 'Bam** down South ('Bam is short for Alabama); **Russians** a southern African American up North ('rushed up here', hence a Russian); **dickty** dodgy, fake, dubious.

SLANG TALK MAN	He gave her his most killing look and let it simmer.
SWEET BACK	S'pose you and me go inside the café here and grab a hot.

Music underscore ends.

GIRL	You got any money?	320
SLANG TALK MAN	The girl asked and stiffed like a ramrod.	
GIRL	Nobody ain't pimping on me. You dig me?	
SWEET BACK AND JELLY	Aww now baby!	
GIRL	I seen you two mullet-heads before. I was uptown when **Joe Brown** had you all in the **go-long** last night. That cop sure hates a pimp. All he needs to see is the pimps' salute and he'll out with his night-stick and **ship your head to the red**. Beat your head just as flat as a dime.	325

330 |

The girl sounds off like a siren. Sweet Back and Jelly rush to silence her.

SWEET BACK	Ah-ah-ah, let's us don't talk about the law. Let's talk about us. About you goin' inside with me to holler, 'Let one come flopping! One come grunting! Snatch one from the rear!'	335
GIRL	Naw indeed. You **skillets** is trying to promote a meal on me. But it'll never happen, brother. You barking up the wrong tree. I wouldn't give you air if	340

Joe Brown the police; **go-long** gaol, lock-up; **ship your head to the red** crack your skull so that it bleeds; **skillets** ship's cooks (i.e. a lowly job).

---

you was stopped up in a jug. I'm not
putting out a thing. I'm just like the
cemetery. I'm not putting out, I'm
takin' in. Dig. I'll tell you like the   345
farmer told the potato – plant you
now and dig you later.

Music underscore.

SLANG TALK MAN   The girl made a movement to switch
off. Sweet Back had not **dirtied a
plate** since the day before. He made   350
a weak but desperate gesture.

*Just as Sweet Back places his hand on her
purse, the girl turns to stare him down. Music
underscore ends.*

GIRL   Trying to snatch my pocketbook, eh?

SLANG TALK MAN   Instead of running . . .

The girl grabs Sweet Back's zoot-suit jacket.

GIRL   How much split you want back here?
If your feets don't hurry up and take   355
you 'way from here, you'll ride away.
I'll spread my lungs all over New York
and call the law.

Jelly moves in to try and calm her.

Go ahead. Bedbug! Touch me! I'll
holler like a pretty white woman!   360

*The girl let out three 'pretty white woman'
screams and then struts off. Music
underscores her exit.*

---

dirtied a plate eaten.

SLANG TALK MAN	She turned suddenly and rocked on off, her earring snapping and her heels popping.
SWEET BACK	My people, my people.
SLANG TALK MAN	Jelly made an effort to appear that he had no part in the fiasco.
JELLY	I know you feel chewed.
SWEET BACK	Oh let her go. When I see people without the periodical principles they's supposed to have, I just don't fool with 'em. *(calling out after her)* What I want to steal her old pocketbook with all the money I got? I could buy a beat chick like you and give you away. I got money's mammy and Grandma's change. One of my women, and not the best one I got neither, is buying me ten shag suits at one time.

He glanced sidewise at Jelly to see if he was convincing.

JELLY	But Jelly's thoughts were far away.

Music underscore.

SLANG TALK MAN	He was remembering those full hot meals he had left back in Alabama to seek wealth and splendor in Harlem without working. He had even forgotten to look cocky and rich.
BLUES SPEAK WOMAN	*I GIT TO THE GIT WITH SOME PAIN AND SOME SPIT AND SOME SPUNK*

The lights slowly fade.

365
370
375
380
385

Activities and ideas for rehearsing *Story in Harlem Slang*

The following can be done in any order.

1   Research the period when the story is set. It was a time of mass migration from the Southern states. Find out how and why Harlem became a centre for African Americans. Also find out what laws discriminated against African Americans in 1942.

Research popular music of the time, so that you can decide whether to use recorded music and/or a combination of live and recorded music.

Write up your research findings about life for African Americans in the United States in the 1940s. Compare and contrast it with the experience of people of African Caribbean origin in Britain today.

2   Use the activities in A1: Moving (pages 2–10) and A8: Narrating and Commentating (pages 48–58) to enhance your understanding of how physical transformation and storytelling are fundamental to this piece.

3   In your performance group, improvise scenes to explore use of slang, and how it changes. You could:

- rework *Story In Harlem Slang* using current slang and music
- perform a scene where two characters use slang to exclude or confuse a third character.

4   Prepare a version of the play as a documentary about people who do not have enough to eat and cannot afford to pay the rent. Use this to ensure that you are clear on what the characters want and need.

5   Jelly and Sweet Back banter and fight in a way that is semi-serious. Create a contemporary scene between two young people, but use your understanding of dramatic tension to move the scene from a light-hearted to a serious quarrel.

6   *Essence machines*

This is an exercise that you may have used in your devised work. The steps are as follows:

- Choose a situation that every one in the group knows, perhaps a boring lesson or work, if you have a Saturday or evening job.
- Each person should choose a sound, a movement or gesture and a word or phrase which captures the "essence" of that situation. For a boring lesson, sounds might be a clock ticking slowly; sighs; a voice droning on and on. Movements might be shifting restlessly in a chair; turning to look out of the window; drumming fingers against a desk.
- Put these together and perform your essence machine by repeating the gestures and sounds all at the same time.
- Experiment with how the effect changes by bringing gestures and sounds in one at a time; building and diminishing volume; having all the noises, phrases and gestures in unison.

Now use this technique to create a piece called 'The Ghetto'.

B7: Excerpt from *Nāga-Mandala* by Girish Karnad (1988)

Girish Karnad was born in Matheran near Bombay in 1938. His mother tongue is Konkani, but *Nāga-Mandala* and his other plays are written in his adopted language Kannada. Karnad translates his own work into English. He has written that, 'My generation was the first to come of age after India became independent of British rule [in 1947] . . . This is the historical context that gave rise to my plays and those of my contemporaries.'

Playwrights have always used history and mythology as a means of addressing contemporary themes. The oldest play in this book, *The Oresteia* (pages 49–53) does just that, as did other Ancient Greek tragedies. Many plays have been based on the Hindu mythological cycle, *The Mahabharata*. But *Nāga-Mandala* is not based on classical myth: it is drawn from two oral folk tales from Kanartka, the province of India where Karnad was born.

By intertwining two stories, Karnad creates a piece of theatre that uses the storytelling form to explore the importance of stories in all our lives. It's a perfect image of how stories change and develop as they are passed on – which is what you do every time you interpret a play.

Cast

Man
Flames 1, 2 and 3
New Flame
The Story
Appanna
Rani
Kappanna
Kurudavva
Dog
King Cobra

This excerpt has been adapted so that an ensemble of six can perform it. The following doublings are suggested:

1 Man/Dog
2 The Story
3 Flame 1/Rani
4 Flame 2/Appanna/King Cobra
5 Flame 3/Kappanna
6 New Flame/Kurudavva

Given the origins of the stories, an all-female group would be appropriate but, as you will see, the piece is so stylised that anyone, whether male or female, can perform any character or characters.

The music at the end of the Prologue can be recorded or played/sung by the characters on stage.

PROLOGUE

The inner sanctum of a ruined temple. The idol is broken, so the presiding deity of the temple cannot be identified.

It is night. Moonlight seeps in through the cracks in the roof and the walls.

*A man is sitting in the temple. Long silence. Suddenly, he opens his eyes wide. Closes them. Then uses his fingers to pry open his eyelids. Then he goes back to his original **morose** stance.*

He yawns involuntarily. Then reacts to the yawn by shaking his head violently, and turns to the audience.

MAN   I may be dead within the next few hours.

Long pause.

I am not talking of 'acting' dead. Actually dead. I might die right in front of your eyes.

Pause.

A **mendicant** told me: 'You must keep awake   5
at least one whole night this month. If you can do that, you'll live. If not, you will die on the last night of the month.' I laughed out loud when I heard him. I thought nothing would be easier than spending a night awake.   10

Pause.

I was wrong. Perhaps death makes one sleepy. Every night this month I have been dozing off before even being aware of it. I am convinced

---

morose gloomy.
mendicant a religious man who lives by begging.

I am seeing something with these eyes of mine, only to wake up and find I was dreaming. Tonight is my last chance.

Pause.

For tonight is the last night of the month. Even of my life, perhaps? For how do I know sleep won't creep in on me again as it has every night so far? I may doze off right in front of you. And that will be the end of me.

Pause.

I asked the mendicant what I had done to deserve this fate. And he said: 'You have written plays. You have staged them. You have caused so many good people, who came trusting you, to fall asleep twisted in miserable chairs, that all that abused mass of sleep has turned against you and become the Curse of Death.'

Pause.

I hadn't realized my plays had had that much impact.

Pause.

Tonight may be my last night. So I have fled from home and come to this temple, nameless and empty. For years I have been lording it over my family as a writer. I couldn't bring myself to die a writer's death in front of them.

Pause.

I swear by this absent God, if I survive tonight I shall have nothing more to do with themes,

plots or stories. I **abjure** all story-telling, all
play-acting.   40

Female voices are heard outside the temple. He looks.

Voices! Here? At this time of night? Lights!
Who could be coming here now?

*He hides behind a pillar. Several Flames enter the
temple, giggling, talking to each other in female
voices.*

MAN   I don't believe it! They are naked lamp flames!
No wicks, no lamps. No one holding them.
Just lamp flames on their own – floating in the   45
air! Is that even possible?

FLAME 3   *(addressing Flame 1, which is already in the temple)*
Hello! What a pleasant surprise! You are here
before us tonight.

FLAME 1   That master of our house, you know what a
skinflint he is! He is convinced his wife has a   50
hole in her palm, so he buys all the groceries
himself. This evening, before the dark was even
an hour old, they ran out of *kusbi* oil. The tin
of peanut oil didn't go far. The bowl of castor
oil was empty anyway. So they had to retire to   55
bed early and I was permitted to come here.

Laughter.

FLAME 2   *(sneering) Kusbi* oil! Peanut oil! How disgusting!
My family comes from the coast. We don't
touch anything but coconut oil.

FLAME 1   . . . But at least I come here every night. What   60
about your friend, the kerosene flame? She

---

abjure renounce.

	hasn't been seen here for months. She is one of the first tonight.
FLAME 3	Actually, from today on I don't think I'll have any difficulty getting out . . . and early. 65
	They all laugh.
FLAME 1	Why? What's happened?
	The other Flames giggle.
FLAMES	Tell her! Tell her!
FLAME 3	My master had an old, ailing mother. Her stomach was bloated, her back covered with bed sores. The house stank of cough and 70 phlegm, pus and urine. No one got a wink of sleep at night. Naturally, I stayed back too. The old lady died this morning, leaving behind my master and his young wife, young and juicy as a tender cucumber. I was chased out fast. 75 *(Giggles.)*
FLAME 2	You are lucky. My master's eyes have to feast on his wife limb by limb if the rest of him is to react. So we lamps have to bear witness to what is better left to the dark.
	They all talk animatedly.
MAN	*(to the audience)* I had heard that when lamps 80 are put out in the village, the flames gather in some remote place and spend the night together, gossiping. So this is where they gather!
	A new Flame enters and is enthusiastically greeted.
FLAME 1	You are late. It is well past midnight. 85
NEW FLAME	Ah! There was such a to-do in our house tonight.

FLAMES   What happened? Tell us!

NEW FLAME   You know I have only an old couple in my house. Tonight the old woman finished eating, 90 swept and cleaned the floor, put away the pots and pans, and went to the room in which her husband was sleeping. And what should she see, but a young woman dressed in a rich, new sari step out of the room! The moment 95 the young woman saw my mistress, she ran out of the house and disappeared into the night. The old woman woke her husband and questioned him. But he said he knew nothing. Which started the rumpus. 100

FLAMES   But who was the young woman? How did she get into your house?

NEW FLAME   Let me explain: My mistress, the old woman, knows a story and a song. But all these years she has kept them to herself, never told the 105 story, nor sung the song. So the story and the song were being choked, imprisoned inside her. This afternoon the old woman took her usual nap after lunch and started snoring. The moment her mouth opened, the story 110 and the song jumped out and hid in the attic. At night, when the old man had gone to sleep, the story took the form of a young woman and the song became a sari. The young woman wrapped herself in the sari and 115 stepped out, just as the old lady was coming in. Thus, the story and song created a feud in the family and were revenged on the old woman.

FLAME 1   So if you try to gag one story, another happens. 120

FLAMES	*(all together)* But where are they now, the poor things? . . . How long will they run around in the dark? What will happen to them?
NEW FLAME	I saw them on my way here and told them to follow me. They should be here any moment . . . There they are! The story with the song! 125

The Story, in the form of a woman dressed in a new, colourful sari, enters, acknowledges the enthusiastic welcome from the Flames with a languid wave of the hand and goes and sits in a corner, looking most despondent. The Flames gather around her.

NEW FLAME	Come on. Why are you so despondent? We are here and are free the whole night. We'll listen to you. 130
STORY	Thank you, my dears. It is kind of you. But what is the point of your listening to a story? You can't pass it on.
FLAMES	That's true . . . What can we do? Wish we could help. 135

While the Flames make sympathetic noises, the Man jumps out from behind the pillar and grabs the Story by her wrist.

MAN	I'll listen to you!

The Flames flee helter-skelter in terror. The Story struggles to free herself.

STORY	Who are you? Let me go!
MAN	What does it matter who I am, I'll listen to you. Isn't that enough? I promise you, I'll listen all night! 140

The Story stops struggling. There is a new interest in her voice.

STORY You will?

MAN Yes.

STORY Good. Then let me go.

He does not.

I need my hands to act out the parts.

He lets her go.

There is a condition, however – 145

MAN What?

STORY You can't just listen to the story and leave it at that. You must tell it again to someone else.

MAN That I certainly shall, if I live. But first I must 150 be alive to . . . That reminds me. I have a condition, too.

STORY Yes?

MAN I must not doze off during the tale. If I do, I die. All your telling will be wasted. 155

STORY As a self-respecting story, that is the least I can promise.

MAN All right then. Start. *(suddenly)* But no! No! It's not possible. I take back my word. I can't repeat the story. 160

STORY And why not?

MAN I have just now taken a vow not to have anything to do with themes, plots or acting. If I live, I don't want to risk any more curses from the audience. 165

STORY *(gets up)* Good-bye then. We must be going.

MAN   Wait! Don't go. Please. *(Thinks.)* I suppose I
have no choice. *(to the audience)* So now you
know why this play is being done. I have no
choice. Bear with me, please. As you can see,   170
it is a matter of life and death for me. *(calls out)*
Musicians, please! *(Music begins.)* The Story and
the Song!

*Throughout the rest of the play, the Man and the Story
remain on stage. The Flames too listen attentively
though from a distance.*

(to the Story) Go on.

ACT ONE

*The locked front door of a house with a yard in front of
the house, and on the right, an enormous ant-hill. The
interior of the house – the kitchen, the bathroom as well
as Rani's room – is clearly seen.*

STORY   A young girl. Her name . . . it doesn't matter.   175
But she was an only daughter, so her parents
called her Rani. Queen. Queen of the whole
wide world. Queen of the long tresses. For
when her hair was tied up in a knot, it was as
though a black King Cobra lay curled on the   180
nape of her neck, coil upon glistening coil.
When it hung loose, the tresses flowed, a
torrent of black, along her young limbs, and
got entangled in her silver anklets. Her fond
father found her a suitable husband. The   185
young man was rich and his parents were
both dead. Rani continued to live with her
parents until she reached womanhood. Soon,
her husband came and took her with him to

his village. His name was – well, any common name will do –

MAN   Appanna?

STORY   Appanna.

Appanna enters, followed by Rani. They carry bundles in their arms, indicating that they have been travelling. Appanna opens the lock on the front door of the house. They go in.

APPANNA   Have we brought in all the bundles?

RANI   Yes.

APPANNA   Well, then, I'll be back tomorrow at noon. Keep my lunch ready. I shall eat and go.

Rani looks at him nonplussed. He pays no attention to her, goes out, shuts the door, locks it from outside and goes away. She runs to the door, pushes it, finds it locked, peers out of the barred window. He is gone.

RANI   Listen – please –

She does not know what is happening, stands perplexed. She cannot even weep. She goes and sits in a corner of her room. Talks to herself indistinctly. Her words become distinct as the lights dim. It is night.

. . . So Rani asks him: 'Where are you taking me?' And the Eagle answers: 'Beyond the seven seas and the seven isles. On the seventh island is a magic garden. And in that garden stands the tree of emeralds. Under that tree, your parents wait for you.' So Rani says: 'Do they? Then please, please take me to them – immediately. Here I come.' So the Eagle carries her clear across the seven seas . . .

She falls asleep. Moans 'Oh, Mother!' 'Father!' in her sleep. It gets light. She wakes up with a fright, looks around, then runs to the bathroom, mimes splashing water on her face, goes into the kitchen, starts cooking. Appanna comes. Opens the lock on the front door and comes in. Goes to the bathroom. Mimes bathing, then comes to the kitchen and sits down to eat. She serves him food.

RANI   Listen – *(fumbling for words)* Listen – I feel – frightened – alone at night –

APPANNA   What is there to be scared of? Just keep to   210
yourself. No one will bother you. Rice!

Pause.

RANI   Please, you could –

APPANNA   Look, I don't like idle chatter. Do as you are
told, you understand? *(Finishes his meal, gets up.)*
I'll be back tomorrow, for lunch.   215

Appanna washes his hands, locks her in and goes away. Rani watches him blankly through the window.

STORY   And so the days rolled by.

Mechanically, Rani goes into the kitchen, starts cooking. Talks to herself.

RANI   Then Rani's parents embrace her and cry.
They kiss her and caress her. At night she
sleeps between them. So she is not frightened
any more. 'Don't worry,' they promise her.   220
'We won't let you go away again ever!' In the
morning, the stag with the golden antlers
comes to the door. He calls out to Rani. She
refuses to go. 'I am not a stag,' he explains, 'I
am a prince'. . .   225

Rani sits staring blankly into the oven. Then begins to sob. Outside, in the street, Kappanna enters, carrying Kurudavva on his shoulders. She is blind. He is in his early twenties.

KAPPANNA Mother, you can't do this! You can't start meddling in other people's affairs the first thing in the morning. That Appanna should have been born a wild beast or a reptile. By some mistake, he got human birth. He can't stand other people. Why do you want to tangle with him?

KURUDAVVA Whatever he is, he is the son of my best friend. His mother and I were like sisters. Poor thing, she died bringing him into this world. Now a new daughter-in-law comes to her house. How can I go on as though nothing has happened? Besides, I haven't slept a wink since you told me you saw Appanna in his concubine's courtyard. He has got himself a bride – and he still goes after that harlot?

KAPPANNA I knew I shouldn't have told you. Now you have insomnia – and I have a backache.

KURUDAVVA Who's asked you to carry me around like this? I haven't, have I? I was born and brought up here. I can find my way around.

KAPPANNA Do you know what I ask for when I pray to Lord Hanuman of the Gymnasium every morning? For more strength. Not to wrestle. Not to fight. Only so I can carry you around.

KURUDAVVA *(pleased)* I know, I know.

Suddenly Kappanna freezes.

What is it? Why have you stopped?

He doesn't answer. Merely stands immobile and stares.
A touch of panic in Kurudavva's voice.

What is it, Kappanna? Kappanna!

KAPPANNA Nothing, Mother. It's just that I can see 255
Appanna's front door from here.

KURUDAVVA *(relieved)* Oh! For a moment I was worried it
was that – who-is-that-again? That witch or
fairy, whatever she is – who you say follows
you around. 260

KAPPANNA Mother, she is not a witch or a fairy. When I try
to explain, you won't even listen. And then,
when I'm not even thinking of her, you start
suspecting all kinds of –

KURUDAVVA Hush! Enough of her now. Tell me why we 265
have stopped.

KAPPANNA There doesn't seem to be anyone in
Appanna's house. There is a lock on the front
door.

KURUDAVVA How is that possible? Even if he is lying in his 270
concubine's house, his bride should be home.

KAPPANNA Who can tell about Appanna? He's a lunatic . . .

KURUDAVVA You don't think he could have sent his wife
back to her parents already, do you? Come, let
us look in through the window and check. 275

KAPPANNA Of course not, Mother! If someone sees us –

KURUDAVVA Listen to me. Go up to the house and peep in.
Tell me what you see.

KAPPANNA I refuse.

KURUDAVVA *(tearful)* I wouldn't have asked you if I had eyes. 280
I don't know why God has been cruel to me,
why he gave me no sight . . .

KAPPANNA	*(yielding)* All right, Mother.

They go near the house. Kappanna peers through the window.

KAPPANNA	The house is empty.	
KURUDAVVA	Of course it is, silly! How can anyone be inside when there is a lock outside on the door? Tell me, can you see clothes drying inside? What kind of clothes? Any saris? Skirts? Or is it only men's clothes?	285
KAPPANNA	I can't see a thing!	290
RANI	Who is it? What is that outside?	
KAPPANNA	Oh my God!	

Lifts Kurudavva and starts running.

KURUDAVVA	Stop! Stop, I tell you! Why are you running as though you've seen a ghost?	
KAPPANNA	There is someone inside the house – a woman!	295
KURUDAVVA	You don't have to tell me that! So what if there is a woman inside the house? We have come here precisely because a woman is supposed to be in the house.	300
KAPPANNA	Mother, what does it mean when a man locks his wife in?	
KURUDAVVA	You tell me.	
KAPPANNA	It means he does not want anyone to talk to his wife.	305
RANI	*(comes to the window)* Who is it?	
KAPPANNA	Let's go.	

Starts running again. Kurudavva hits him on the back.

KURUDAVVA	Stop! Stop! *(to Rani)* I am coming, child! Right now! Don't go away! *(to Kappanna)* He keeps his wife locked up like a caged bird? I must talk to her. Let me down – instantly. 310

He lets her down.

You go home if you like.

KAPPANNA	I'll wait for you here under the tree. Come back soon. Don't just sit there gossiping . . .
KURUDAVVA	*(approaching Rani)* Dear girl . . . 315
RANI	Who are you?
KURUDAVVA	Don't be afraid. I am called Kurudavva, because I am blind. Your mother-in-law and I were like sisters. I helped when your husband was born. Don't be frightened. Appanna is like a son to me. Is he not in? 320
RANI	No.
KURUDAVVA	What is your name?
RANI	They call me Rani.
KURUDAVVA	And where is Appanna? 325
RANI	I don't know.
KURUDAVVA	When did he go out?
RANI	After lunch yesterday.
KURUDAVVA	When will he come back?
RANI	He will be back for lunch later in the day. 330
KURUDAVVA	You don't mean, he is home only once a day, and that too . . . only for lunch?

No reply.

And you are alone in the house all day?

Rani begins to sob.

	Don't cry child, don't cry. I haven't come here to make you cry. Does he lock you up every day like this? 335
RANI	Yes, since the day I came here . . .
KURUDAVVA	Does he beat you or ill-treat you?
RANI	No.
KURUDAVVA	*(pause)* Does he . . . 'talk' to you? 340
RANI	Oh, that he does. But not a syllable more than required. 'Do this', 'Do that', 'Serve the food.'
KURUDAVVA	You mean – ? That means – you are – still – hmm! Has he . . . ?
RANI	Apart from him, you are the first person I have 345 seen since coming here. I'm bored to death. There is no one to talk to!
KURUDAVVA	That's not what I meant by 'talk'. Has your husband touched you? How can I put it? *(exasperated)* Didn't anyone explain to you 350 before your wedding? Your mother? Or an aunt?
RANI	Mother started shedding tears the day I **matured** and was still crying when I left with my husband. Poor her! She is probably crying 355 even now. *(Starts sobbing.)*
KURUDAVVA	Dear girl, it's no use crying. Don't cry! Don't! Come here. Come, come to the window. Let me touch you. My eyes are all in my fingers. *(She feels Rani's face, shoulder, neck through the bars of the window.)* Ayyo! How beautiful you are. Ears 360 like **hibiscus**. Skin like young mango leaves. Lips like rolls of silk. How can that Appanna

---

matured reached puberty; **hibiscus** a flowering bush.

gallivant around leaving such loveliness
wasting away at home?

RANI   I am so frightened at night, I can't sleep a   365
wink. At home, I sleep between Father and
Mother. But here, alone – Kurudavva, can you
help me, please? Will you please send word to
my parents that I am, like this, here? Will you
ask them to free me and take me home? I   370
would jump into a well – if only I could –

KURUDAVVA   Chih! Chih! You shouldn't say such things. I'll
take care of everything. *(calls out)* Son! Son!

KAPPANNA   *(from behind the tree)* Yes?

KURUDAVVA   Come here.   375

KAPPANNA   No, I won't.

KURUDAVVA   Come here, you idiot.

KAPPANNA   I absolutely refuse, Mother. I told you right at
the start that I won't.

KURUDAVVA   Honestly! *(Comes to him.)* Listen, Son. Run   380
home now. Go into the cattle shed – the left
corner –

KAPPANNA   The left corner –

KURUDAVVA   Just above where you keep the plough,
behind the pillar, on the shelf –   385

KAPPANNA   Behind the pillar – on the shelf –

KURUDAVVA   There is an old tin trunk. Take it down. It's full
of odds and ends, but take out the bundle of
cloth. Untie it. Inside there is a wooden box.

KAPPANNA   A wooden box. All right –   390

KURUDAVVA   In the right hand side of the wooden box is a
coconut shell wrapped in a piece of paper.
Inside are two pieces of a root. Bring them.

KAPPANNA	Now?

KURUDAVVA   Now. At once. Before Appanna returns   39●
home.

KURUDAVVA   Don't waste time now. Do as I say. Run.

Gets up and comes back to the house. Kappanna leaves.

Are you still there?

RANI   Yes. Who is that?

KURUDAVVA   My son, Kappanna. Oh, don't let his name   40●
mislead you. He isn't really dark. In fact, when
he was born, my husband said: 'Such a fair
child! Let's call him the Fair One!' I said: 'I
don't know what Fair means. My blind eyes
know only the dark. So let's call this little   40●
parrot of my eyes the Dark One!' And he
became Kappanna.

RANI   And where have you sent him?

KURUDAVVA   I'll tell you. I was born blind. No one would
marry me. My father wore himself out going   41●
from village to village looking for a husband.
But to no avail. One day a mendicant came to
our house. No one was home. I was alone. I
looked after him in every way. Cooked hot
food specially for him and served him to his   41●
heart's content. He was pleased with me and
gave me three pieces of a root. 'Any man who
eats one of these will marry you,' he said.

RANI   And then?

KURUDAVVA   'Feed him the smallest piece first,' he said. 'If   42●
that gives no results, then try the middle-sized
one. Only if both fail, feed him the largest
piece.'

RANI	*(entranced)* And then?
KURUDAVVA	One day a boy distantly related to me came to 425 our village and stayed with us. That day I ground one of the pieces into paste, mixed it in with the food, and served him. Can you guess which piece I chose?
RANI	*(working it out)* Which one now? The smallest 430 one, as the mendicant said? No, no, surely the biggest piece.
KURUDAVVA	No, I was in such a hurry I barely noticed the small one. The biggest scared me. So, I used the middle-sized root. 435
RANI	And then?
KURUDAVVA	He finished his meal, gave me one look and fell in love. Married me within the next two days. Never went back to his village. It took the plague to detach him 440 from me.

Rani laughs.

KAPPANNA	*(entering)* Mother –
KURUDAVVA	Ha! There he is! Wait! *(Goes to him.)* Have you brought them?

*Kappanna gives her the two pieces of root. Kurudavva
hurries back to Rani.*

	Are you still there? 445
RANI	Yes, I am.
KURUDAVVA	Here.
RANI	What is that?
KURUDAVVA	The root I was telling you about.

Rani starts.

	Here. Take this smaller piece. That should do for a pretty jasmine like you. Take it! Grind it into a nice paste and feed it to your husband. And watch the results. Once he smells you he won't go sniffing after that bitch. He will make you a wife instantly.
RANI	But I am his wife already.
KURUDAVVA	Just do as I say.

<margin>450</margin>
<margin>455</margin>

Rani takes the piece. Kurudavva tucks the other one in the knot of her sari. Kappanna whistles. She turns.

That must be Appanna coming.

RANI	*(running in)* Go now, Kurudavva. But come again.
KURUDAVVA	I shall too. But don't forget what I told you.

<margin>460</margin>

Kurudavva starts to go. Appanna crosses her.

APPANNA	*(suspicious)* Who is that? Kurudavva?
KURUDAVVA	How are you, Appanna? It's been a long time –
APPANNA	What are you doing here?
KURUDAVVA	I heard you had brought a new bride. Thought I would talk to her. But she refuses to come out.
APPANNA	She won't talk to any one. And no one need talk to her.
KURUDAVVA	If you say so. *(Exits.)*
APPANNA	*(so she can hear)* I put a lock on the door so those with sight could see. Now what does one do about blind meddlers? I think I'll keep a watch dog. *(Opens the door and goes in. To Rani.)* I am lunching out today. I'll have my bath and go. Just heat up a glass of milk for me.

<margin>465</margin>
<margin>470</margin>

Goes into the bathroom. Mimes bathing. Rani boils the milk. Pours it in a glass and starts to take it out. Notices the piece of root. Stops. Thinks. Runs out. Sees that he is still bathing. Runs back into the kitchen, makes a paste of the root.

APPANNA *(dressing)* Milk! 475

Rani jumps with fright. Hurriedly mixes the paste into the milk. Comes out and gives Appanna the glass of milk. He drinks it in a single gulp. Hands the glass back to her. Goes to the door, ready to put the lock on. She watches him intently. He tries to shut the door. Suddenly clutches his head. Slides down to the floor. Stretches out and goes to sleep on the door-step, half inside and half outside the house. Rani is distraught. Runs to him. Shakes him. He doesn' t wake up. He is in a deep sleep. She tries to drag him into the house, but he is too heavy for her. She sits down and starts crying.

APPANNA *(groggily)* Water! Water!

She brings a pot of water. Splashes it on his face. He wakes up slowly, staggers up. Washes his face. Pushes her in. Locks the door from outside. Goes away. Rani watches, stunned. Slowly goes back to her bedroom. Starts talking to herself. It becomes night.

RANI . . . So the demon locks her up in his castle. Then it rains for seven days and seven nights. It pours. The sea floods the city. The waters break down the door of the castle. Then a big 480 whale comes to Rani and says: 'Come, Rani, let us go . . .'

She falls asleep. Midnight. Kappanna enters carrying Kurudavva. Stumbles on a stone. They fall.

KURUDAVVA Thoo! That's the problem with having eyes: one can't see in the dark. That's why I have

	been telling you to let me go on my own at least at night –
KAPPANNA	Go! Go! From this point on you can certainly go alone. I refuse to come any closer to that house. And what are you doing, Mother? Suppose he is in the house. And he hears you. What will you say? That you have come to gossip with his wife in the dead of night?
KURUDAVVA	Shut up! We are here only to find out if the lock is gone yet. If it's gone, he is inside now. That means success is ours. We'll leave right away. *(Goes and touches the door. It is closed. Tip-toes to feel the latch. The lock is still there. Recoils in surprise.)* I can't believe it. The lock is still there. *(Thinks.)* Perhaps he has taken her out to the fields or the garden! *(Laughs)*
RANI	*(wakes up)* Who is that?
KURUDAVVA	Me.
RANI	*(comes running)* Who? Kurudavva? This time of the night?
KURUDAVVA	What happened, child? Why is the lock still there?
	No reply.
	Did you feed him the root?
RANI	Yes.
KURUDAVVA	And what happened?
RANI	Nothing. He felt giddy. Fainted. Then got up and left.
KURUDAVVA	That's bad. This is no ordinary infatuation then. That concubine of his is obviously –

485

490

495

500

505

510

RANI	Who?

KURUDAVVA	Didn't want to tell you. There is a woman, a 515 bazaar woman. She has your husband in her clutches. Squeezes him dry. Maybe she's cast a spell. There is only one solution to this –

RANI	What?

KURUDAVVA	*(giving her the bigger piece)* Feed him this larger 520 piece of root.

RANI	No!

KURUDAVVA	Yes!

RANI	That little piece made him sick. This one –

KURUDAVVA	It will do good, believe me. This is not hearsay. 525 I am telling you from my own experience. Go in. Start grinding it. Make a tasty curry. Mix the paste in it. Let him taste a spoonful and he will be your slave. And then? Just say the word and he will carry you to my house himself. 530

Rani blushes.

Son! Son! *(to Rani)* Remember. Don't let
anything frighten you.

*Rani goes into the kitchen. Kurudavva wakes up
Kappanna. They exit. It gets brighter. Appanna comes.
He has a vicious-looking dog on a chain with him. He
brings it to the front yard and ties it to a tree stump there.
Then comes to the front door and unlocks it. The dog
begins to bark. Surprised at the bark, Rani peers out of
the window.*

RANI	Oh! A dog –

APPANNA	That blind woman and her son! Let them step here again and they'll know – ! I'll bathe and 535 come to eat. Serve my food.

Goes to the bathroom and starts bathing. Rani takes down her pot of curry. Removes the lid. Takes out the paste of the root.

RANI   *(to the Story)* Shall I pour it in?

Appanna calmly continues his bath. It is evident he has heard nothing.

Oh my god! What horrible mess is this? Blood. Perhaps poison. Shall I serve him this? That woman is blind, but he isn't. How could he possibly not see this boiling blood, this poisonous red? And then – even if he doesn't see it – how do I know it is not dangerous? Suppose something happens to my husband? What will my fate be? That little piece made him ill. Who knows . . . ? *(Slaps herself on her cheeks.)* No, no. Forgive me, God. This is evil. I was about to commit a crime. Father, Mother, how could I, your daughter, agree to such a **heinous** act? No, I must get rid of this before he notices anything.   550

She brings the pot out. Avoids the husband in the bathroom. Steps out of the house. Starts pouring out the curry. Stops.

RANI   No! How awful! It's leaving a red stain. He is bound to notice it, right here on the doorstep! What shall I do? Where can I pour it, so he won't see?

STORY   Rani, put it in that ant-hill.   555

RANI   Ah, the ant-hill!

Runs to the tall ant-hill. Starts pouring the liquid into it. The dog starts howling in the front yard.

---

heinous very shameful.

APPANNA	Rani! See what is bothering the dog! *(surprised at receiving no reply)* Rani! Rani!

Goes to the kitchen, drying himself. She is not there. Comes to the front door looking for her. By this time Rani has poured the curry into the ant-hill and is running back to the house. The moment she turns her back to the ant-hill, a King Cobra lifts its hood, hissing, out of the ant-hill. Looks around. It sees Rani and follows her at a distance. By the time she has reached the front door of her house, it is behind a nearby tree, watching her.

Rani comes to the front door and freezes. Appanna is waiting for her.

APPANNA	Rani, where have you been?

No answer.

I said, where have you been? Rani, answer me! 560

Moves aside so she can go in. But the moment she steps in, Appanna slaps her hard. Rani collapses to the floor. He does not look at her again. Just pulls the door shut, locks it from outside and goes away. There is not a trace of anger in anything he does. Just cold contempt. The dog barks loudly at the King Cobra which watches from behind the tree, hissing, excited, restless. Appanna goes away. Rani goes to her bedroom. Throws herself down in her usual corner, crying.

It gets dark.

The King Cobra is still watching from under the tree. The dog continues to bark.

When it is totally dark, the Cobra moves toward the house. The barking becomes louder, more continuous. Rani wakes up, goes to the window, curses and shouts. Goes back to bed. The Cobra enters the house through the drain in the bathroom.

STORY   As you know, a cobra can assume any form it likes. That night, it entered the house through the bathroom drain and took the shape of –

The Cobra takes the shape of Appanna. To distinguish this Appanna from the real one, we shall call him Naga, meaning a 'Cobra'.

Naga searches for Rani in the house. Finds her sleeping in the bedroom. Watches her.

Activities and ideas for rehearsing *Nāga-Mandala*

1   AK Ramanujan, a famous collector of folk tales, has written that:

Even in a large modern city like Madras, Bombay or Calcutta, even in the western-style nuclear families with their well-planned 2.2 children, folklore . . . is only a suburb away, a cousin or a grand-mother away.

Ask the older members of your family to tell you the stories that they remember being told when they were young. Share these with the other performers in your group.

2   The Flames get together for a gossip and a chat. Improvise a realistic scene involving gossip, to give you ideas about the tone of voice they use and to help you create different characters.

3   To explore the dynamic between Rani and her husband Appanna, improvise a scene that puts the relationship in a contemporary British context and situation.

4   Storytelling and transformation are fundamental conventions of *Nāga Mandala*. Use the following activities in Section A as part of your rehearsal process:

- A1: Moving (pages 2–11)
- A8: Narrating and Commentating, expecially Activities 3 (page 54) and 5 (page 57)

- A11: Emoting, expecially the activities which explore magnifying (page 89)

5 *Nāga Mandala* creates a world where many characters are not human. List all these, for instance:

- The Story
- Flames
- Dog
- King Cobra.

Use what you know about physicalising and transformation to create appropriate movements for each of these. You might also wish to think about whether the house is represented by people and if so, how to stage this!

5 To create an appropriate style for the piece, try having all the actors on stage all the time. Discuss and experiment with how you will make it clear when and how they step in and out of the action. Also, decide how you will make it clear when the characters are addressing the audience and when they are talking to each other. How will you use music and sound to underscore the action and heighten the dream-like atmosphere?

6 In the early twenty-first century there are many urban myths, such as the vanishing hitch-hiker who turns out to be a ghost or the take-away restaurant that serves fried rat, rather than fried chicken. These are usually stories that are supposed to have happened to a friend of a friend. Compare notes on which urban myths you have heard. Then write one as a play, using the storytelling and transformation principles that are used in *Nāga-Mandala*.

Acknowledgements

The publishers gratefully acknowledge the following for permission to reproduce copyright material. Every effort has been made to trace or contact copyright holders, but in some cases has proved impossible. The publishers would be happy to hear from any copyright holder that has not been acknowledged.

Extract from 'Gum and Goo' from *Plays for a Poor Theatre* by Howard Benton published by Methuen. Reprinted with permission of Methuen Publishing Limited. Applications for amateur performances should be addressed in the first instance to Casarotto Ramsay & Associates Limited, National House, 60-66 Wardour Street, London W1V 4ND tel 020 7287 4450

Extract from *Bouncers* by Jon Godber, Originally published by Josef Weinberger Limited (pka Warner/Chappell Plays Limited) Copyright © 1987, 1993 by John Godber. This edition published by permission of Josef Weinberger Limited. Applications for amateur performances (excluding North America) should be addressed to Josef Weinberger Limited, 12-14 Mortimer Street, London W1T 3JJ tel 020 7580 2827

Extract from *Under Milk Wood* by Dylan Thomas, published by J M Dent, Reprinted by permission of David Higham Associates Limited. Applications for amateur performances should be addressed in the first instance to David Higham Associates Limited, 5-8 Lower John Street, Golden Square, London W1F 9HA tel 020 7437 7888

Extract from *Long Day's Journey into the Night* by Eugene O'Niell, published by Jonathan Cape. Reprinted by permission of the Random House Group Limited. Application for amateur performances should be directed to the Random House Group Limited who will refer you elsewhere if necessary

Extract from *Kiss Me Like You Mean It* by Chris Chibnall, published by Oberon Books Limited. Reprinted by permission of Oberon Books Limited. Application for amateur performances should be directed to Oberon Books limited tel 020 7607 3637 who will refer you elsewhere if necessary

Extract from *Blithe Spirit* by Noel Coward, published by Methuen. Reprinted by permission of Methuen Publishing Limited. Applications for amateur performances should be addressed in the first instance to Alan Brodie Representation Limited, 211 Piccadilly, London W1V 9LD tel 020 7917 2871

Extract from *My Sister in This House* by Wendy Kesselman, published by Samuel French. Copyright © 1982 by Wendy Kesselman. Applications for amateur performances should be addressed to William Morris Agency Inc, 1325 Avenue of the Americas, New York, NY 10019, USA tel 001 212 903 1155 fax 001 212 903 1426

Extract from *Ooh Ah Showab Khan* by Clifford Oliver, published by Carel Press 1997. Reprinted by permission of Arc Theatre, London. Applications for amateur performances should be addressed in the first instance to Arc Theatre , London fax: 020 8594 1052

Extract from *And Then There Were None* by Agatha Christie, Copyright © 1944 by Samuel French Limited, Copyright © 1972 in renewal by Agatha Christie. Reprinted with permission of Chorion (IP) Limited. Applications for amateur performances should be addressed in the first instance to Intellectual Properties, Chorion (IP) Limited, Vernon House, Shaftesbury Avenue, London W1D 7ER tel 020 7434 1880

Extract from *Fool for Love* by Sam Shepard, published by City Lights Books, USA 1983 and Faber and Faber UK. Reprinted by permission of City Lights Books USA. Applications for amateur performances should be addressed in the first instance to Faber and Faber Limited, tel 020 7465 0045 who will refer you elsewhere if necessary

Extract from 'Scapin the Schemer' from *Don Juan and Other Plays* by Molière, translated by George Gravely and Ian Maclean, published by Oxford University Press, UK. Reprinted with the permission of Oxford University Press. Applications for amateur performances should be addressed in the first instance to Oxford University Press tel 01865 556767 who will refer you elsewhere if necessary

Extract from *The Oresteia* by Aeschylus, translated by Ted Hughes, published by Faber and Faber in 1999. Reprinted with permission of the publishers. Applications for amateur performances should be addressed in the first instance to Faber and Faber Limited, tel 020 7465 0045 who will refer you elsewhere if necessary

Extract from *Nana/Germinal* by Zola, translated by Olwen Wymark, published by Oberon Books Limited. Reprinted by permission of Oberon Books Limited. Applications for amateur performances should be addressed to The Agency, 24 Pottery Lane, London W11 4LZ tel 020 7727 1346

Extract from *Far Away* by Caryl Churchill. Copyright © Caryl Churchill 2000 reproduced by courtesy of Nick Hern Books, The Glasshouse, 49a Goldhawk Road, London W12 8QP email info@nickhernbooks.demon.co.uk. Applications for amateur performances should be addressed to Casarotto Ramsay & Associates Limited, National House, 60-66 Wardour Street, London W1V 4ND tel 020 7287 4450

Extract from *Rope* by Patrick Hamilton, published by Constable & Co 1929. Reprinted by permission of Contable & Robinson Limited. Applications for amateur performances should be addressed to A. M. Heath & Co. Ltd., 79 St. Martin's Lane, London WC2N 4AA tel 020 7836 4271

Extract from *Landscape of the Body* by John Guare Copyright © 1978 by St. Jude Publications, Inc. Reprinted by permission of Kay Collyer & Boose LLP on behalf of the author. Applications for amateur performances should be addressed to Kay Collyer & Boose LLP, One Dag Hammarskjold Plaza, New York, NY 10017-2299, USA tel 001 212 940 8200

Extract from *Soft Cops* by Caryl Churchill, published by Methuen. Reprinted by permission of Methuen Publishing Limited. Applications for amateur performances should be addressed to Casarotto Ramsay & Associates Limited, National House, 60-66 Wardour Street, London W1V 4ND tel 020 7287 4450

Extract from 'Execution of Justice' from *Testimonies: Four Plays* by Emily Mann. Copyright © 1997 by Emily Mann. Published by Theatre Communications Group. Used by permission of Theatre Communications Group, Inc. Applications for amateur performances should be addressed to Theatre Communications Group Inc, 355 Lexington Avenue, New York, NY 10017-0217 tel 001 212 697 5230

Extract from *Woyzeck* by George Büchner, translated by Michael Patterson, published by Methuen. Reprinted by permission of Methuen Publishing Limited. Applications for amateur performances should be addressed to Methuen Publishing Limited tel 020 7233 9827 who may refer you elsewhere if necessary

The Actor's Nightmare by Christopher Durang, reprinted by permission of Helen Merrill Limited. *The Actor's Nightmare* was first presented by Playwrights Horizons in New York City, On October 14th, 1981. The production was directed by Jerry Zaks. The final performance was January 29th, 1984. Applications for amateur performances should be addressed to Helen Merrill Limited, 295 Lafayette Street, Suite 915, New York NY 10012

Extract from 'Linda Her' from *Linda Her and the Fairy Garden* by Harry Kondoleon. Copyright © 1985 by Harry Kondoleon. Applications for amateur performances should be addressed to William Morris Agency Inc, 1325 Avenue of the Americas, New York, NY 10019, USA tel 001 212 903 1155 fax 001 212 903 1426

Extract from 'Harlem Slang' from *Spunk: Three Tales* by Zora Neale Hurston, adapted by George C. Wolfe, Copyright © 1989, 1990, 1991 by George C. Wolfe, published by Theatre Communications Group. Used by permission of Theatre Communications Group Inc. Applications for amateur performances should be addressed to Theatre Communications Group, Inc, 355 Lexington Avenue, New York, NY 10017-0217 tel 001 212 697 5230

Extract from *Nāga Mandala* by Girish Karnad, Act One – Prologue, published by Oxford University Press, India. Reprinted by permission of Oxford University Press, New Delhi, India. Applications for amateur performances should be directed to Oxford University Press, YMCA Library Building, Jai Singh Road, New Delhi 110001, India tel 91 11 3747124 fax 91 11 336 0897/374 2312;